Educational Games for Fun

EDUCATIONAL GAMES *for Fun*

Margaret E. Mulac

HARPER & ROW, PUBLISHERS

New York, Evanston, San Francisco, London

STANDARD BOOK NUMBER: 06-013099-7

LIBRARY OF CONGRESS CATALOG CARD NUMBER: 77-138752

Designed by Yvette A. Vogel

Dedicated to
Great-nieces Alisa and Reneé Sauvageot,
great-nephews Kevin, Owen, and Brian Gross,
and Benjamin K. Hoffmann who arrived just in
time to be included,
and
my young neighbors the "cookie pickers"
of Scarborough Road

Contents

Acknowledgments

An author of game books finds materials everywhere. An idea here, a suggestion there, a question in an almanac—all may help to set off a whole new line of thinking and give birth to a group of new games.

My gratitude to persons known and unknown and especially to those teachers who contributed to "Teaching Tips" in the *Grade Teacher* magazine. Will they recognize their ideas in some of the games, I wonder?

Foreword

An educational game book by its very nature deals with the
subjects that make up a normal school program—spelling, arithmetic, geography, science, history, and language. All these
subjects are important components of the school curriculum:
it is important to learn to read; it is necessary to know about
arithmetic and mathematics to live fully in this complex world;
geography, history, science, and other subjects are necessary
if a child is to take his place in the world of the future. But while
it is important to acquire knowledge and develop particular
skills, it is just as vital to learn how to use one's knowledge and
skills for fun and enjoyment. It is an invaluable lesson learned
when one finds that mental gymnastics can be as much fun as
physical sports. It is important to know, too, that because a
game makes us think, that does not make it less a game or less
fun than an activity that does not require or challenge the
mental processes.

For this author-recreation leader, it is not enough to teach
children to read, spell, speak well, work sums, solve math problems, or memorize historical, geographical, or scientific facts.
It is also necessary to employ play methods that make skills

developed in school so much fun to use that they will become a part of leisure-time activities. In other words, it is not only important to know how to read, it is important to know that it is fun to read. The better our reading skills, the more kinds of reading materials will bring pleasure, joy, relaxation, or inspiration.

When normal study work becomes fun, an important barrier is hurdled. Learning takes on new meaning and importance. Chores become challenges. The disciplines of study seem less burdensome. The senses through which we learn become more acute. Awareness, without which life is dull and colorless, is developed, opening new doors to enrichment. Facts learned through games are no less informative, no less accurate. Skills developed through play methods are as valuable assets to the individual as those acquired through scholastic methods. More— educational games are tools in education for leisure, a commodity modern man has in greater supply than man in any other age. If education is to be complete, it cannot neglect this vital responsibility. It is not enough to educate for the purposes of making a living. We must also educate to help make a life.

The games included here are thinking games. They deal with words, spelling, arithmetic, history, and geography. To some they may look more like work than play. But this could be said of golf, swimming, dancing, playing a guitar, or building a tree house. It is the method of approach that makes work into play. The teacher will note that in game directions the children are always called players rather than pupils. It is hoped that many will find the games more fun than work.

For most of the games, considerable reference material has been prepared to aid the teacher. In word games dealing with homonyms, for example, long lists of qualifying words have been given so that the teacher has a ready list for suggestion or for checking but they are by no means comprehensive ones.

This was done not only for the convenience of the teacher but to indicate that more than one play period can be spent on a specific word problem. The same game can be played many times without exhausting the list of words in that particular category. Too, many games include variations so that they may be repeated with a slightly different twist.

Similarly, in the history or geography games reference material important to the game is given to eliminate the necessity of going to other references to check answers. And to make the task of the teacher easier, the game directions are written to be read to the class so that the teacher can familiarize herself with the game as she reads it aloud.

The games have been graded on a flexible basis, the reference materials including examples for young as well as older children. But since the teacher knows her classes better than anyone else, she will make the final determination as to which games best fit her groups and will select the examples from the reference lists most suitable for them.

Many games have been suggested as team games in which players can pool their ideas and consolidate their talents. The interplay in this kind of situation is often as valuable as the game itself, and acts to enhance it. Certainly it makes a thinking game seem most unlike a test, in which seeking help from others is not exactly the accepted form.

Finally, this book introduces its own form of "new math," for which the author takes full responsibility, trusting that it will not set education back fifty years.

And so, to the games. Have fun!

MARGARET E. MULAC

I.

ARITHMETIC *and* MATHEMATICAL GAMES

Arithmetic and math skills can be used just for fun—and no one will be unhappy, either, if such skills are further developed through play. The math and arithmetic games introduced here do more than challenge the math "brain." They may make spelling an important part of a problem, or they may implant an idea through proverbs or other words of wisdom. Sometimes the problems themselves may seem ridiculous, but the answers will require serious concentration and accuracy and application of skills. If you are required to add two apples, three bananas, and four oranges, and divide by three children, the answer will not be an empty fruit bowl! Players will learn that three plus four, played by the "new math" rules, adds up to nine. Hopefully, they will also find that arithmetic can be fun.

It is hoped, too, that the games will be so intriguing that the players will make up their own ridiculous math problems, bring them into class, and challenge their classmates.

So, take a class, add an arithmetic game, divide by concentration, subtract boredom, and come up with fun.

CRAZY MATHEMATICS

Type of Game: Spelling-arithmetic   *Grades:*   4 and up
Play Method: Individual written

Read a series of numbers, which the players are to spell out and write, one under the other. When they have finished writing, they should count the number of letters in each word and put that number out to the right of the word. Then tell them how to use the numbers in the problem. This is one instance when seventy plus eighty equals thirteen!

seventy	7
eighty	+ 6
Answer	13

Reading Directions

This is a spelling-arithmetic game. I will read you a series of numbers, which you will spell out and write, one under the other. When you have finished writing the words, count the letters in each word you have written and write the number out to the right of each word. Like this example on the blackboard:

twenty	6		
thirty	× 6	36	
two	÷ 3	12	
sixteen	− 7		
Answer		5	

Note: Write the problem on the board without the signs. Fill those in when you come to that part in the reading directions which deals with them and work the problem to demonstrate.

When everyone is ready, I will tell you what to do with each number in working out the problem. Of course, if you haven't spelled a word right you will have a hard time getting the right answer. You have a chance, however, even if you misspell a word, providing you have used the right number of letters in the

word. You may still be able to get the math part correct. Lucky
flukes are part of every game. It's like hitting a baseball on the
handle of the bat and getting a Texas League hit. So let's see
how we come out. Try to spell every word correctly—you can't
always be lucky. We will score a point for a correct answer and
an extra point for spelling the words correctly. Ready?

Teacher Reference List (Spelling Problems)

1.			
	eleven	6	
	seven	+ 5	11
	six	× 3	33
	three	− 5	
	Answer		28

2.			
	seventy	7	
	ninety-one	× 9	63
	sixty-six	− 8	55
	forty-four	+ 9	64
	fourteen	÷ 8	
	Answer		8

3.			
	twenty-seven	11	
	forty-three	× 10	110
	sixteen	+ 7	117
	twenty-six	÷ 9	13
	thirty-two	− 9	
	Answer		4

4.			
	sixty-eight	10	
	forty-nine	× 9	90
	seventeen	+ 9	99
	fifteen	− 7	92
	twelve	× 6	
	Answer		552

5.			
	ninety-nine	10	
	seventy-two	× 10	100
	fifty-one	+ 8	108
	twenty-three	− 11	97
	sixty-six	× 8	776
	five	÷ 4	
	Answer		194

6.			
	forty-three	10	
	thirteen	+ 8	18
	twelve	× 6	108
	seventeen	÷ 9	12
	sixty-three	× 10	
	Answer		120

7.			
	fifty-five	9	
	sixty-three	× 10	90
	forty-four	+ 9	99
	seventy-six	× 10	990
	ninety-seven	÷ 11	90
	fourteen	− 8	
	Answer		82

8.			
	sixty-six	8	
	seventy-seven	+ 12	20
	fifty-five	× 9	180
	forty-four	÷ 9	20
	nine	+ 4	
	Answer		24

9.			
	twenty-one	9	
	thirty-two	+ 9	18
	forty-four	× 9	162
	fifty-five	− 9	153
	sixty-six	+ 8	
	Answer		161

10.	seventy-seven	12	
	eighty-eight	+ 11	23
	ninety-nine	× 10	230
	one hundred	− 10	220
	zero	÷ 4	
	Answer		55

11.	twelve	6	
	eleven	× 6	36
	ten	÷ 3	12
	nine	× 4	48
	fifteen	+ 7	55
	eight	÷ 5	
	Answer		11

12.	ten	3	
	eleven	× 6	18
	twelve	+ 6	24
	thirteen	÷ 8	3
	fourteen	+ 8	
	Answer		11

13.	one thousand	11	
	one hundred	× 10	110
	one million	+ 10	120
	one billion	÷ 10	12
	one zero	− 7	
	Answer		5

14.	one hundred one	13	
	ninety-two	× 9	117
	eighty-one	+ 9	126
	seventy	÷ 7	18
	sixty-nine	− 9	
	Answer		9

15.			
two hundred		10	
four thousand	+	12	22
sixteen hundred	×	14	308
seven million	−	12	296
two zeros	÷	8	
Answer			37

16.			
forty-seven		10	
fifty-eight	+	10	20
sixty-nine	×	9	180
seventy-one	−	10	170
eight	÷	5	
Answer			34

17.			
one hundred		10	
divided by	+	9	19
fourteen	×	8	152
subtract	+	8	160
nine	÷	4	40
add ten	−	6	
Answer			34

Note: Encourage players to make up problems at home with which they can challenge the class at future game periods.

Variation #1: Problems can be made up on the spot if an answer in fractions is desired. This, of course, depends upon the age and abilities of the players. An example employing fractions follows:

sixteen		7	
divided by	×	9	63
nineteen	−	8	55
plus seven	+	9	64
minus fourteen	÷	13	
Answer			$4\frac{12}{13}$

Variation #2:   Problems may be made more difficult by raising numbers to the power of two or more and dividing by square roots of others. Such problems must be worked out in advance. An example follows:

sixty-two	8	
multiplied by	$\times$ 12	96
fourteen	$- 8^2$	32
subtract	$\div$ 8	4
plus sixteen	$+ 11$	
Answer		15

DICE ARITHMETIC

Type of Game: Number recognition   Grades: Kindergarten, 1, and up

To teach children to recognize numbers quickly, make sets of dice from building blocks. Number each of the six sides of each die by pasting contact-paper numbers 1 through 6 over the other designs on the blocks.

With young children divide the players into groups, giving each group one die. The players take turns rolling the die and calling out the number on top. The player rolling must call out the number quickly.

With older children, give each group two dice. The player must call out both numbers. Or, regular dice may be used. In this case a player must count the number of pips and then call out the sum.

Reading Directions

Many games we will play as we get older will use little square blocks with pips or spots on them. They are called dice. If you have only one of the blocks, it is called a die. The dice can help us learn our numbers as we play this game, since each side of a die has a different number on it. Since the die has six sides there will be six numbers, 1, 2, 3, 4, 5, and 6. We have made our own dice from building blocks today, with the numbers printed on them rather than pips.

I will show you how the game goes. Pretend that it is my turn to roll the die. I roll it on the table like this. See, the number showing on top is a 5, so I will say "Five." I then give the die to the next player, who takes his turn and then tells the number he sees on top.

Let's see how fast we can play and still tell the right numbers.

DICE MATHEMATICS

Type of Game: Math   Grades: 2 and up
Play Method: Team

Organize your class into groups of no more than six players and give each team a pair of regular dice. Play may be on a table or level desk for each team or on the floor. Each team should have a captain, who keeps a score sheet.

Reading Directions

Many familiar games such as parchesi, Cootie, or Bunco are played with dice. Today we will use dice for a mathematical game. Each player in turn will roll the dice once. On the first time around, each player will add the pips or spots on the dice and call out the answer. If he gives the right answer, the captain scores a point for his team. The dice go to the next player, who takes his turn, and so on. After each player has had his turn, we will check the score to see which team has the most points.

On the second time around, the players will subtract the smaller number from the larger and call out the answer. The scoring method is the same. On the third time around, the numbers on the pips will be multiplied. On the fourth round, the method will be division. On the fifth round we will use only one die and the players must square the number.

At the beginning of each round I will announce the method you are to be using, whether it is to be adding, subtracting, or whatever. The team with the highest score at the end of the game wins. Ready?

Note: Whether or not you use the square root round depends upon the age of the children, of course.

Variation #1: With older players two dice can be used, the players squaring the total of pips rolled.

Variation #2: With older players, a third die may be added to the game. In the subtraction round, the player adds the total of two dice and subtracts the third. The choice of which to add and which to subtract is his, but he must make it clear to his team what he is doing before he gives his answer. In the division roll round, a player adds the totals of two dice and divides by the third. Again the decision as to which he adds and by which he divides is his to make. In squaring the numbers, he may add the total and square it or he may square each number and add the total of the numbers squared. The choice is his, but again he must tell his team which method he is using so that each can work the problem with him.

Variation #3: Make your own dice of large wooden blocks and write numbers from 1 through 6 on one, and 7 through 12 on the second and let the players name the methods to be used on each roll.

A simple way is to use regular building blocks. Cover with contact paper on which pips have been marked to resemble dice.

MATHEMATICAL WEATHER PREDICTIONS

Type of Game: Spelling-arithmetic   *Grades:* 4 and up
Play Method: Individual written

Read the prophecy, line by line, the players writing the lines
as dictated. When all have finished writing, the players should
add the number of letters in each line and put that number
out to the side. When all are ready, tell the players what to
do with each number. For example, the prophecy might be:

Rain before	10	
seven	+ 5	15
stop	× 4	60
before eleven.	÷ 12	
Answer		5

To get a correct answer, a player must be able to spell as
well as work the problem. However, sometimes a misspelled
word may have the correct number of letters, so a player might
still get a correct answer. Score a point for a correct answer and
an extra point if all the words are correctly spelled.

Reading Directions
This is a spelling-arithmetic game that tells us how people pre-
dicted the weather long ago before there were weathermen
and meteorologists. I will read a weather prediction, a line at a
time. You will write it as I read it, writing one line under
the other. See how the one on the board is written. Spell the
words carefully. This is important to your answer. When you
have finished writing, count the number of letters in each line

and write the number after each line. When everyone is ready, I will tell you what to do with each number. Sometimes you will multiply, sometimes add, subtract, or divide the numbers. Now you see why it is important to spell the words correctly. If you misspell a word, you may not have the right number of letters, so you cannot work out the problem correctly. There is a chance, however, that you might misspell a word but still have the right number of letters in it. In that case you could get the right answer to the arithmetic problem. So, we will score a point for a correct answer and an extra point for spelling all the words correctly.

I hope you will remember the weather proverb, too. Next time you see a certain kind of sky or notice a wind from a particular direction, it will be fun to see if the old proverb is as good a predictor as your local weatherman.

Teacher Reference List (Weather Prediction Problems)

1.	Red sky at night	13	
	is a sailors'	+ 10	23
	delight.	− 7	16
	Red sky	× 6	96
	in the morning	÷ 12	8
	is a sailors'	× 10	80
	warning.	− 7	
	Answer		73
2.	Rain before	10	
	seven	+ 5	15
	stop	× 4	60
	before eleven.	÷ 12	
	Answer		5

3. Mackerel 8
   scales + 6 14
   and × 3 42
   mares' tails + 10 52
   make ÷ 4 13
   lofty ships × 10 130
   carry ÷ 5 26
   low sails. + 8
   _____
   Answer 34

4. Summer's white clouds 18
   with high − 8 10
   mushroom towers + 14 24
   are signs ÷ 8 3
   to be ready + 9 12
   for quick × 8 96
   sudden showers. − 13
   _____
   Answer 83

5. When the 7
   dew is + 5 12
   on the grass, × 10 120
   rain will ÷ 8 15
   never come + 9 24
   to pass. ÷ 6
   _____
   Answer 4

6. When the glass 12
   falls low, + 8 20
   prepare × 7 140
   for a blow. − 8 132
   When it ÷ 6 22
   rises high − 9 13
   let all your × 10 130
   kites fly. + 8
   _____
   Answer 138

7. (American Indian)

When the		7	
locks turn	×	9	63
damp in the	+	9	72
scalp house,	×	10	720
surely it	÷	8	90
will rain.	−	8	
Answer			82

8.

The weather		10	
and the moon	+	10	20
may change	+	9	29
together	−	8	21
but the change	×	12	252
of the moon	÷	9	28
does not change	+	13	41
the weather.	×	10	
Answer			410

9.

If the groundhog		14	
sees his shadow	+	13	27
on February two,	+	13	40
six more weeks	+	12	52
of winter's cold	÷	13	4
is due.	×	5	
Answer			20

Note: Encourage players to make up problems at home with which they can challenge the others at future game periods.

Variation #1: Problems can be made more difficult by using square roots and raising some numbers to the power of two or more. The last problem is repeated using this method as an example.

If the groundhog		14	
sees his shadow	+	13	27
on February two,	+	13^2	196
six more weeks	+	12	208
of winter's cold	÷	13	16
is due.	×	5	
Answer			80

Variation #2: Where fractions are within the range of abilities and knowledge, problems can be made up almost on the spot. Again using the same problem, the example shown employs use of fractions.

If the groundhog		14	
sees his shadow	×	13	182
on February two,	+	13	195
six more weeks	÷	12	16¼
of winter's cold	−	13	3¼
is due.	×	5	
Answer			16¼

MIXED MEASURE ARITHMETIC

Type of Game: Arithmetic   Grades: 4 and up
Play Method: Individual written

Read a problem to the players, who will attempt to work it out. Players should raise hands as they finish.

Reading Directions

This is a tricky arithmetic game dealing with all kinds of units of measure such as inches, gallons, and dozens, with some other funny kinds thrown in for the fun of it. For example, a problem might sound like this:

Take the number of sticks in a pack of gum	5
Multiply by the number of nickels in a quarter	5
	25
Add the number of players on a baseball team	9
	34
Add the number of pints in a quart	2
	36

Divide by the number of inches in a foot (12) and give me the answer.

Answer	3

Let's see if you can work the problems without becoming too confused. Remember 2 and 2 is 4 even if it is oranges and nickels, pints and feet, or bubble gum and baseball players. Ready?

Teacher Reference List (Mixed Measure Arithmetic)

1. Take the number of pounds in half a ton	1000
Multiply by the number of feet on a dog	4000
Divide by the number of nickels in a dollar	200
Subtract the number of inches in a foot	188
Divide by the number of quarts in a gallon.	
Answer	47
2. Take the number of oranges in a dozen	12
Multiply by the number of inches in a yard	432
Subtract the number of dimes in a dollar	422
Divide by the number of pints in a quart.	
Answer	211

3. Take the number of pennies in a dollar   100
   Multiply by the number of thirds in a circle   300
   Divide by the number of inches in a foot of string   25
   Subtract the number of nickels in a quarter.

   Answer   20

4. Take the pennies in a quarter of a dollar   25
   Add the number of inches in a yard of wieners   61
   Subtract the number of players on a football team   50
   Subtract the number of minutes in half an hour   20
   Divide by the number of nickels in a dime.

   Answer   10

5. Take the number of little pigs in the story   3
   Multiply by the number of minutes in an hour   180
   Divide by half a dozen bananas   30
   Subtract the number of blackbirds baked in a pie   6
   Add the number of wheels on a bicycle.

   Answer   8

6. Take the number of days in September   30
   Multiply by the fingers on your left hand   150
   Divide by the number of eyes a cat has   75
   Subtract the number of days in a week   68
   Add the number of strings on a violin.

   Answer   72

7. Take the number of weeks in a year   52
   Subtract the number of minutes in half an hour   22
   Divide by the number of players on a soccer team   2
   Multiply by the number of legs on a cat.

   Answer   8

8. Take the number of toes on both feet   10
   Multiply by the number of pints in a quart   20
   Add the number of months in half a year   26
   Subtract the number of thumbs on two hands   24
   Divide by a dozen oranges.
                                                                          ___
   Answer   2

9. Take the number of wheels on a tricycle   3
   Multiply by the number of days in February in a leap year   87
   Add the number of inches in a half yard of ribbon   105
   Divide by the number of toes on your right foot.
                                                                          ___
   Answer   21

10. Take the number of quarts in a gallon of ice cream   4
    Add the number of feet in a yard of calico   7
    Multiply by the number of ounces in half a pound
       of macaroni   56
    Divide by the number of pints in half a gallon of vinegar.
                                                                          ___
    Answer   14

11. Take the number of hours in a day   24
    Divide by half a dozen pears   4
    Multiply by two pairs of scissors   8
    Subtract one nickel   7
    Add a quarter-dozen boxes of popcorn.
                                                                          ___
    Answer   10

12. Take the number of ears on a dog   2
    Multiply by the number of feet on that same dog   8
    Add two cans of dog food   10
    Divide by the number of eyes the dog has   5
    Subtract the number of tails the dog has.
                                                                          ___
    Answer   4

13. Take the number of days in April   30
    Add a half dozen umbrellas   36
    Divide by the number of inches in half a foot of rain   6
    Multiply by the number of sneezes in a quarter-dozen.
                                                                    ___
    Answer   18

14. Take the number of feet in four yards of spaghetti   12
    Add the number of ounces in half a pound of
      spaghetti sauce   20
    Add the number of ounces in a pound of meat   36
    Divide by the number of mouths in three-quarter-dozen
      hungry children.
                                                                    ___
    Answer   4

15. Take the year Columbus discovered America   1492
    Divide by a third-dozen Indians   373
    Subtract the number of days in a leap year   7
    Multiply by the number of ships in Columbus's fleet   21
    Add the number of hours in half a day.
                                                                    ___
    Answer   33

16. Take the number of school days in a week   5
    Multiply by two dozen school children   120
    Add a principal and a sixth-dozen teachers   123
    Subtract the ears on two custodians.
                                                                    ___
    Answer   119

17. Take the number of states in the U.S.   50
    Multiply by the number of colors in our flag   150
    Divide by Hawaii and Alaska (2 states)   75
    Subtract the number of Carolinas and Dakotas   71
    Add Virginia and West Virginia.
                                                                    ___
    Answer   73

18. Take the number of hands on a clock   2
    Multiply by the number of numerals on the face   24
    Add the number of minutes in half an hour   54
    Subtract the number of hours in a day.

Answer   30

Note: Encourage players to work out problems at home to use in future game periods.

Variation #1: If the concept of fractions is known to players, many problems can be made up almost on the spur of the moment, since coming out even is not then a necessary factor. An example follows:

Take one banana	13	
peel slowly	+ 10	23
eat carefully	× 12	276
in four bites	− 11	265
swallowing after	÷ 15	17⅔
each bite.	+ 8	
Answer		25⅔

Variation #2: Problems can be made more difficult by using square roots and raising numbers to the power of two or more. An example follows:

Take one	7	
trick and treat bag	× 16	112
fill full	+ 8	120
with assorted	÷ 12	10
goodies	+ 7^2	59
empty into	− $\sqrt{9}$	56
one child	÷ 8	7
end with sick.	× 11	
Answer		77

NURSERY RHYME ARITHMETIC

Type of Game: Spelling-arithmetic   *Grades:*   4 and up
Play Method: Individual written

Read a nursery rhyme a line at a time to the players, who should write them down, one line under the other. When the writing is completed, the players should count the letters in each line and put that number out to the right of the line. When all are ready, tell the players what to do with each number. The correct answer to the problem depends upon correct spelling, except when a player misspells a word but uses the correct number of letters; he may still get the right answer. Lucky goofs are part of any game. Give a point for a correct answer and an extra point if all words are correctly spelled.

Reading Directions

This is a spelling-arithmetic game that uses nursery rhymes. I will read a line of a rhyme and you will write it, being careful of your spelling, since this is an important part of the game. You will write one line under another as I read it. When you have all finished writing, you will add the number of letters in each line you have written and put that number out to the right of each line. Look at the example I have written on the blackboard. Then I will tell you what sign to put in front of each number to make an arithmetic problem.

A tisket	7	
a tasket	+ 7	14
a green	− 6	8
and yellow	× 9	72
basket	÷ 6	
Answer		12

You can see why your spelling is so important. If you misspell a word, you will not get the right answer. There is an exception, however. You may misspell a word but still get the right number of letters in it. In that case, you could get the right answer to the arithmetic problem. So, we will give a point for the right answer and an extra point if all your words are spelled correctly.

So let's see how well you can spell and how accurately you can work your problems. Ready?

Teacher Reference List

1. Star light   9
   star bright   × 10   90
   first star   + 9   99
   I see tonight.   ÷ 11   9
   I wish I may   + 9   18
   I wish I might   × 11   198
   have the wish   − 11   187
   I wish tonight.   + 12

   Answer   199

2. Jack Sprat could   14
   eat no fat   + 8   22
   his wife could   + 12   34
   eat no lean,   − 9   25
   so between   × 9   225
   the two of them   − 12   213
   they licked   × 10   2130
   the platter   − 10   2120
   clean.   ÷ 5

   Answer   424

3. One   3
   two   +   3   6
   button   ×   6   36
   your   −   4   32
   shoe   ÷   4

   Answer   8

4. Three   5
   four   +   4   9
   close   ×   5   45
   the   ÷   3   15
   door   −   4

   Answer   11

5. Five   4
   six   ×   3   12
   pick up   ÷   6   2
   sticks   +   6

   Answer   8

6. Seven   5
   eight   +   5   10
   keep   −   4   6
   them   ×   4   24
   straight   ÷   8

   Answer   3

7. Nine   4
   ten   ×   3   12
   a big   ×   4   48
   fat   ÷   3   16
   hen   −   3

   Answer   13

8. Eleven   6
   twelve   × 6   36
   miners   − 6   30
   do   ÷ 2   15
   delve   + 5

   Answer   20

9. Lucy   4
   Locket   × 6   24
   lost   × 4   96
   her   ÷ 3   32
   pocket   − 6

   Answer   26

10. Rich man   7
    poor man   × 7   49
    beggar man   − 9   40
    thief   ÷ 5   8
    doctor   × 6   48
    lawyer   − 6   42
    Indian chief   + 11

    Answer   53

11. I find it   7
    hard to   × 6   42
    multiply   + 8   50
    to divide is   ÷ 10   5
    just as bad   × 9   45
    and adding   + 9   54
    and subtracting − 14   40
    nearly drive   × 11   440
    me mad!   ÷ 5

    Answer   88

12.	If ifs and ands	12	
	were pots	+ 8	20
	and pans	× 7	140
	there'd be	− 8	132
	no need	÷ 6	22
	for tinkers.	× 10	
	Answer		220

13.	Jack be nimble	12	
	Jack be quick	+ 11	23
	Jack jump over	× 12	276
	the candle stick.	− 14	
	Answer		262

14.	Chairs to mend	12	
	old chairs	+ 9	21
	to mend	− 6	15
	mackerel	× 8	120
	fresh mackerel	− 13	107
	any old rags?	× 10	
	Answer		1070

15.	Thirty days	10	
	hath September	× 13	130
	April, June and	+ 12	142
	November	+ 8	150
	all the rest	÷ 10	15
	have thirty-one	+ 13	28
	except February alone	− 19	9
	and that has	× 10	90
	twenty-eight	× 11	990
	days clear	÷ 9	110
	And twenty-nine	+ 13	123
	in each	− 6	117
	leap year.	+ 8	
	Answer		125

16. There was   8
    an old lady   × 9   72
    swallowed a fly   − 13   59
    I don't know   − 9   50
    why she   × 6   300
    swallowed a fly,   − 13   287
    the poor old lady. + 14

    Answer   301

17. Billy had a   9
    monkey   + 6   15
    who climbed upon × 14   210
    a stick   ÷ 6   35
    fed the monkey   − 12   23
    too much candy   × 12   276
    made the   − 7   269
    monkey sick!   × 10

    Answer   2690

18. There was   8
    an old   + 5   13
    woman   × 5   65
    lived under   + 10   75
    a hill   ÷ 5   15
    if she's not   + 9   24
    gone   ÷ 4   6
    she lives   + 8   14
    there still.   × 10

    Answer   140

Note: Encourage players to make up problems at home with which they can challenge players at future game periods.

Variation #1: Where the inclusion of fractions in a problem

is desirable and within the limits of the players, problems can be made up almost on the spot. An example follows:

A tisket		7
a tasket	× 7	49
a green	+ 6	55
and yellow	÷ 9	$6\frac{1}{9}$
basket.	− 6	
Answer		$\frac{1}{9}$

Variation #2: Problems can be made more difficult by using square roots or raising numbers to the power of two or more. An example follows:

There was		8
a crooked	+ 8	16
man	× 3^2	144
who walked	÷ $\sqrt{9}$	48
a crooked	− 8	40
mile.	× 4^2	
Answer		640

PROVERBIAL PROBLEMS

Type of Game: Spelling-arithmetic   Grades: 3 and up
Play Method: Individual written

Read the proverb line by line. The players should write it as dictated, one line at a time. When all have finished writing, the players should count the number of letters in the words of each line and put the total at the end of the line. For example, take the proverb "A stitch in time saves nine." It would be written in this manner and the number of letters in each line written to the side:

A stitch	7	
in time	× 6	42
saves	− 5	37
nine.	+ 4	
Answer		41

When the players have finished their writing and counting, tell them what to do with the numbers. Obviously, the correct answer cannot be obtained if the words are misspelled, unless a writer misspells a word but uses the correct number of letters. In this instance, if he worked the problem correctly, he would end with the correct answer. But happy accidents are part of any game—a golfer may flub his shot, hit a tree, and land on the green or a batter can get a broken-bat hit. In scoring, give an extra point for correctly spelled words as well as a point for a correct answer.

Reading Directions

Our game today is a spelling-arithmetic game. I will read you a proverb, a line at a time. You will write it one line under the other. Look at the example on the board. When you have finished writing, count the letters in the words of each line and write that number out to the side as it is done on the blackboard. When you are ready, I will tell you what signs to put in front of each number to make it into a problem. As soon as you have worked the problem, stand. Let's see who gets finished first with the right answer.

The trick to this game is that if you can't spell the words correctly you probably won't get the right answer. And yet, if you have misspelled a word but used the right number of letters, you may still get the right answer. So if you are the first up and your answer is correct, you will score a point. But I may ask you to spell the words as you have written them. If the words are correctly spelled, you will get an extra point. Ready?

Teacher Reference List of Proverbial Problems (Grades 3 through 6)

1. Penny		5	
in pocket	×	8	40
is	÷	2	20
good	+	4	24
company.	−	7	
Answer			17

2. Rolling		7	
stones	×	6	42
gather	−	6	36
no	÷	2	18
moss.	+	4	
Answer			22

3. The day		6	
has eyes	×	7	42
the night	+	8	50
has ears.	−	7	
Answer			43

4. That		4	
which is	×	7	28
well done	−	8	20
is done	×	6	120
twice.	÷	5	
Answer			24

5. Send   4

a fool	+ 5	9
to market	+ 8	17
a fool	− 5	12
he will	× 6	72
return.	÷ 6	
Answer		12

6. Pay   3

what you owe	× 10	30
and you will	+ 10	40
know what	÷ 8	5
is your own.	+ 9	
Answer		14

7. When the well   11

is dry	+ 5	16
we know	× 6	96
the worth	÷ 8	12
of water.	− 7	
Answer		5

8. Those   5

who are feared	× 12	60
are	÷ 3	20
hated.	+ 5	
Answer		25

9. Nature is loved   13

by what	× 6	78
is best	− 6	72
in us.	÷ 4	
Answer		18

10. If a man
    has faith
    in his power
    he can
    wait.

    Answer

		6	
has faith	+	8	14
in his power	×	10	140
he can	÷	5	28
wait.	−	4	
Answer			24

11. A penny
    saved
    is a
    penny earned.

    Answer

		6	
saved	×	5	30
is a	÷	3	10
penny earned.	+	11	
Answer			21

12. Early to bed
    early to rise
    makes a man
    healthy, wealthy,
    and wise.

    Answer

		10	
early to rise	×	11	110
makes a man	+	9	119
healthy, wealthy,	−	14	105
and wise.	÷	7	
Answer			15

13. An empty bag
    cannot
    stand
    upright.

    Answer

		10	
cannot	×	6	60
stand	÷	5	12
upright.	+	7	
Answer			19

14. When
    in doubt
    mind your own
    business.

    Answer

		4	
in doubt	+	7	11
mind your own	×	11	121
business.	−	8	
Answer			113

15. Be silent
    or speak
    something
    worth hearing.

            8
    ×   7   56
    +   9   65
    − 12
    _____
    Answer   53

16. He that can
    have patience
    can have
    what he will.

            9
    + 12   21
    ÷   7   3
    × 10
    _____
    Answer   30

17. One today
    is worth
    two
    tomorrows.

            8
    +   7   15
    ÷   3   5
    ×   9
    _____
    Answer   45

18. A poor
    example
    is the
    best sermon.

            5
    ×   7   35
    ÷   5   7
    + 10
    _____
    Answer   17

19. Promises may
    get you friends
    but nonperformance
    will turn them
    into enemies.

           11
    + 13   24
    × 17   408
    ÷ 12   34
    − 11
    _____
    Answer   23

20. There are   8
    lazy minds   × 9   72
    as well as   + 8   80
    lazy bodies.   ÷ 10

    Answer   8

21. You   3
    may delay   + 8   11
    but time   × 7   77
    will not.   − 7

    Answer   70

22. Tell me   6
    my faults   + 8   14
    and mend   × 7   98
    your own.   − 7

    Answer   91

23. Well done   8
    is better   × 8   64
    than   ÷ 4   16
    well said.   + 8

    Answer   24

24. No   2
    gains   × 5   10
    without   + 7   17
    pains.   − 5

    Answer   12

25. Every time   9
    a sheep   × 6   54
    blats   − 5   49
    it loses   ÷ 7   7
    a mouthful.   + 9

    Answer   16

26. It is better   10
    to be silent   × 10   100
    and be thought   − 12   88
    a fool   ×   5   440
    than to speak   ÷ 11   40
    and remove   ×   9   360
    the doubt.   −   8
                       _____
    Answer   352

27. Knowledge   9
    in youth   ×   7   63
    is wisdom   −   8   55
    in age.   ÷   5
                       _____
    Answer   11

28. Pride   5
    goes before   × 10   50
    and shame   −   8   42
    follows   ÷   7   6
    after.   +   5
                       _____
    Answer   11

29. A forced   7
    kindness   +   8   15
    deserves   ×   8   120
    no thanks.   −   8
                       _____
    Answer   112

30. A good cause   10
    makes   ×   5   50
    a stout heart   + 11   61
    and a   −   4   57
    strong arm.   ÷   9
                       _____
    Answer   6⅓

31.	A good		5	
	beginning	+	9	14
	makes a	×	6	84
	good	÷	4	21
	ending.	−	6	
	Answer			15

32.	A good		5	
	name	+	4	9
	is better	×	8	72
	than	÷	4	18
	riches.	−	6	
	Answer			12

33.	A little		7	
	knowledge	×	9	63
	is a	÷	3	21
	dangerous	+	9	30
	thing.	−	5	
	Answer			25

Note: Suggest that players work out problems at home with which to challenge others at future game periods.

Variation #1: Most problems have been worked out without fractions. By changing a sign here and there, fractions can be brought into the problems. An example problem is treated to be worked with and without fractions:

Every man		8		Every man		8	
has a	× 4	32		has a	+ 4	12
fool	+ 4	36		fool	÷ 4	3
in his	÷ 5	7⅕		in his	+ 5	8
sleeve.	− 6			sleeve.	× 6	
Answer		1⅕		Answer		48

Variation #2. Problems can be made more difficult by squaring some numbers and by asking for square roots of others. An example follows:

Experience		10^2	
is the father	$\times$	11	1100
of wisdom,	$+$	8^2	1164
and memory	$\div$	$\sqrt{9}$	388
the mother.	$-$	9	
Answer			379

Variation #3. The first or any number can be multiplied by 10 and the problem proceed in the usual manner. An asterisk after the number indicates that it is to be multiplied by 10. An example follows:

Every scrap		10*	
of a	$\times$	3	300
wise man's time	$+$	12*	420
is worth	$\div$	7	60
saving.	$+$	6*	
Answer			120

TRICKY ARITHMETIC

Type of Game: Number counting   Grades: 3 and up
Play Method: For two players

Read the solution first so that you will know how to play and win the game before teaching it. The solution is given here so the teacher can win every time until the players begin to learn some of the tricks. Do not give the solution to the players, but let them work it out as they play. Once everybody knows the trick, the game is no fun.

Younger players will play this by the guess, hope, and luck method. Older players will soon realize that if you can work your opponent down to five, he can't win. It may take some time for the math wizards to work it down to the final solution.

Solution

There are fifteen playing pieces to begin with. These may be lines drawn on a piece of paper and crossed off, or lines drawn on the blackboard and erased to the final conclusion. They may be bottle caps or other small items.

The game is to draw one, two, or three pieces alternately with an opponent. The player who is left to take the last piece loses the game.

The trick numbers are 2, 6, 10. If you know the solution you can win every time. By taking two on the first move the game is already won, but your opponent is happily unaware of this: no matter how many pieces he takes on his move, you can take the sixth piece. For example, you take two, he takes three. You take one and that makes the sixth piece taken. Then again, no matter how many the opponent takes, you can make the total drawn ten. This leaves five. No matter how many your opponent takes, you can take enough to leave the last for him.

Older players will soon discover that if it is your move and you are left with five, you can't win. It will take them longer to work the solution back to the tricky first move.

In demonstrating the game before the class, draw fifteen lines on the blackboard. Play against a volunteer. Erase lines or cross them off as they are chosen. You, the teacher, begin the first game by taking two. You will win, of course. The volunteer gets a second chance. Let him play first. He may also take two on his first move, but since he does not know the trick, you can still beat him. On your first move in the third game, confuse the issue and take only one. If you play according to the trick, you may still get either the sixth or the tenth and work it down to the impossible five.

Once the players understand the game, pair them off and let them play against each other, taking turns to be first at the start of each new game.

Reading Directions

This is a trick number game. At first we will play with fifteen lines on the blackboard. I will play against a volunteer and you watch to see how the game is played. We will take turns taking one, two, or three lines. As they are taken, I will erase them from the board. The player who has to take the last one loses the game. Watch carefully—I take two (*erase two from the blackboard*). My opponent takes how many? Three? Very well, I will take one. He takes two. Okay, I take two. He takes one? I will take three and that leaves him with one and I win.

Let's give him another chance to play. It is hard to learn the game on the first try. It is his turn to play first. (*Continue through the second game. Then play a third game.*)

I think you all understand how the game is played. Try to leave one line for your opponent and you can win. We will now pair off. Each two will play with paper and pencil. (*If you have bottle caps or some other playing pieces to use, the game is more fun.*)

Variation #1:   This is similar to the original Tricky Arithmetic game in that there are fifteen playing pieces. Again the player tries to leave the last piece for his opponent. But there are two differences:

1. The fifteen pieces are divided into three groups, as:

/ / /	/ / / / /	/ / / / / / /
Group 1	Group 2	Group 3

2. A player can take any number on any move so long as he takes them from one group only. Thus, the first player might take all seven of group 3, leaving only groups 1 and 2. The next player might take all of group 2, but this would be foolish as the first player need only take two from group 1 and leave the last piece for his opponent. What looks so easy is really tricky. Some of the winning combinations to work toward are two groups of four as:

	/ / / /	/ / / /
Group 1	**Group 2**	**Group 3**

one in each group as:

/	/	/
Group 1	**Group 2**	**Group 3**

The 4–4 combination can be worked down then to a 3–3 and then a 2–2 combination against which the opponent can do nothing but lose graciously.

Note: Try this game out before teaching it, then teach as a blackboard game so that the whole class can learn at once. Pair off the players and let them go to it. The tricks are left to the players to find out for themselves, of course.

Variation #1:   Use sixteen pieces. The magic numbers are 3, 7, and 11. If you can win the eleventh piece, it leaves the unbeatable five.

Variation #2:   Use twenty pieces. The magic numbers are 3, 7, 11, and 15. If you can win the fifteenth piece, it again leaves the unbeatable five.

Variation #3:   Arrange the sixteen pieces into three groups of 3, 6, and 7. Play according to the rules of variation #1.

Variation #4:   Arrange twenty-one pieces into three groups of 5, 7, and 9. Play according to the rules of variation #1.

WORD ARITHMETIC

Type of Game: Spelling-arithmetic   Grades: 3 and up
Play Method: Individual written

Read the words to the players, who should write them one under the other. They should then count the number of letters in each word and write the number to the right of the word. Then tell the players how to use the numbers in a problem.

Correct spelling is necessary to get the right answer except when a word is misspelled but the misspelling contains the correct number of letters. Give a point for a correct answer and an extra point if all words are spelled correctly.

Reading Directions

This is a spelling-arithmetic game. I will read you several words, which you will write one under the other. Then you will count the number of letters in each word and write that number out to the right of the word. When everybody is ready, I will tell you the signs to put in front of each number to make the numbers into an arithmetic problem. Of course, if you have not spelled the words correctly you may not get the right number of letters and your answer won't be correct. However, sometimes we misspell a word but use the right number of letters. In that case you could get the correct answer. So, I will give a point for the correct answer and another point if all words are spelled correctly.

Let's do an example on the board so you will all know how the game works.

Note: Write the words first, one under the other and then set the numbers out to the right. Then write in the signs and work the problem.

joke		4	
laugh	×	5	20
giggle	+	6	26
funny	−	5	
Answer			21

Now you see how the game works. Are you ready?

1.
juice		5	
bacon	×	5	25
eggs	×	4	100
toast	÷	5	20
milk	−	4	16
breakfast	+	9	
Answer			25

2.
winter's cold		11	
jacket	×	6	66
mittens	−	7	59
boots and socks	+	13	72
warm	÷	4	
Answer			18

3.
summer		6	
vacation	×	8	48
trip	÷	4	12
enjoy	−	5	7
too short	+	8	
Answer			15

4. money in   7
   pockets   × 7   49
   spend all   + 8   57
   broke   − 5

   Answer   52

5. game   4
   referee   × 7   28
   sportsmanship   − 13   15
   fun   ÷ 3   5
   great sport   + 10

   Answer   15

6. recess   6
   games   + 5   11
   active   × 6   66
   fun   ÷ 3   22
   refreshing   − 10

   Answer   12

7. sled   4
   snow   + 4   8
   coasting   × 8   64
   cold   ÷ 4   16
   home   − 4

   Answer   12

8. hungry   6
   sandwich   × 8   48
   milk   ÷ 4   12
   apple   + 5   17
   full   − 4

   Answer   13

9. playground 10
   fun and games ..... + 11 21
   activity ..... × 8 168
   healthy ..... ÷ 7

   Answer 24

10. street 6
    play ..... + 4 10
    unsafe ..... × 6 60
    hurt ..... ÷ 4 15
    sorrow ..... − 6

    Answer 9

11. dog and cat 9
    fight ..... × 5 45
    barking ..... − 7 38
    and spitting ..... + 11 49
    run home ..... ÷ 7

    Answer 7

12. ham and eggs 10
    bread and butter ..... + 14 24
    taste good ..... × 9 216
    when together ..... ÷ 12

    Answer 18

13. ice cream 8
    and cake ..... + 7 15
    help make ..... × 8 120
    a party ..... ÷ 6

    Answer 20

14. election   8
     vote   ×   4   32
     elect   —   5   27
     democracy   ÷   9
     Answer   ─────────
                                    3

15. boy and glove   11
     baseball   +   8   19
     others   ×   6   114
     good fun   —   7
     Answer   ─────────
                                   107

16. football   8
     kick   ×   4   32
     throw   —   5   27
     run   ÷   3   9
     fun   +   3
     Answer   ─────────
                                   12

17. girl   4
     candy   +   5   9
     friend   ×   6   54
     share   —   5   49
     nothing   ÷   7   7
     remains   —   7
     Answer   ─────────
                                    0

18. bicycle   7
     girl   +   4   11
     ride   ×   4   44
     spill   —   5   39
     cry   ÷   3
     Answer   ─────────
                                   13

19.	school		6	
	study hard	+	9	15
	learn much	×	9	135
	wisdom	−	6	
	Answer			129

20.	mystery		7	
	story	+	5	12
	exciting	−	8	4
	clues	×	5	20
	solve	+	5	
	Answer			25

21.	red and		6	
	yellow	+	6	12
	mixed	×	5	60
	make	÷	4	15
	orange	×	6	
	Answer			90

22.	blue and		7	
	yellow	+	6	13
	mixed	×	5	65
	make	−	4	61
	green	×	5	
	Answer			305

23.	happiness		9	
	is a	×	3	27
	good	−	4	23
	feeling	+	7	30
	inside	÷	6	
	Answer			5

24.			
cake		4	
candles	+	7	11
birthday	×	8	88
children	−	8	80
party	÷	5	
Answer			16

25.			
movie		5	
popcorn	×	7	35
watch	÷	5	7
funny	−	5	2
finish	+	6	8
home	×	4	
Answer			32

Note: Suggest that players work out problems at home with which to challenge the players in future game periods.

Variation #1: In cases where players know fractions, the teacher can quickly work out other problems beforehand since coming out even is not a necessity. An example follows:

tricks		6	
treats	×	6	36
masks	+	5	41
pumpkins	÷	8	5⅛
goblins	×	7	35⅞
Halloween	−	9	
Answer			24⅞

Variation #2: More difficult problems can be devised by raising some numbers to the power of two or more or requiring the square root of others. An example follows:

problem		7	
worked	×	6	42
correctly	÷ $\sqrt{}$	9	14
gives	−	5	9
right	×	5^2	225
answer	+	6	
Answer			231

GUESS WHO IS LAST

Type of Game: Guessing (quiet)   Grades: 1 and up
Play Method: Team

Divide the group into two teams. Select one team to be first. This team decides which member is to be WHO. Then they line up facing the second team and the game begins.

Reading Directions

This is a guessing game for two teams. Team 1 will select one of its members to be WHO and then line up facing team 2. All players on team 1 try to look equally guilty to make it difficult for team 2.

Team 2 players, in turn, try to guess who is WHO and then try not to pick him. The first player on team 2 asks any player on team 1: "Are you WHO?" If that players says he is not WHO, then both the asked and asking players sit down. Then the second player of team 2 takes his turn and tries not to pick WHO.

When WHO is found, the game ends. We count the number of players still standing on team 1 and score that number against team 2. Now team 2 picks a WHO and team 1 tries to pick him last. The team with the lowest score wins.

Variation: Give one team a paper clip to hide in the hand of one player. All line up facing the second team with clenched fists held out in front of them. Players on the second team, in turn, tap a hand. If the hand is empty, the player lowers this hand to his side. When both empty hands of a player have been eliminated, that player sits down. When the paper clip is located, count the number of hands still up and score that number against the guessing team.

II.

HISTORY *and*
GEOGRAPHY
GAMES

GEOGRAPHICAL AND HISTORICAL
WONDER-ABOUTS

Type of Game: Geography or history   *Grades:*   3 and up
Play Method: Oral individual

Present the problem and, after allowing five minutes for the
players to examine maps and jot down odd-sounding names,
ask for volunteers from the class. The game will be more fun if,
after the first time it is introduced, the players do some private
research with geographies, road maps, or zip code directories.
A simple prize might even be awarded to the best lists. Certainly, some truly unbelievable names will be found.

Reading Directions
In plain sight on state maps, in your geography, on road maps,
or in a zip code directory are names of cities and towns that are
unusual and wonderful. Some make you want to say them over
and over again, others make you wonder how they came to be.
Take, for example, Young America, Indiana. Don't you wonder

how it happened to be named that? Or Grand Chain, Illinois. Is it named after a square dance figure, do you suppose? How would you like to tell someone that you lived in Sweet Home, California? Try saying over and over again this musical-sounding combination: Cynthiana, Indiana. You could almost write a song about it.

Some town names are the same as those of distant places. If we went to Indiana we could go to Rome, Peru, Carthage, Montezuma, New Paris, Russiaville, Scotland, Valparaiso, Versailles, Warsaw, Waterloo, and for the fun of it we could end up in Tell City.

Today, let's see how many towns and cities with odd names we can think of. I know we will find animals (Buffalo, New York), birds (Eagle, Alaska), faraway places (Rome, New York), just funny-odd names (Bimble, Kentucky), and even names of occupations (Umpire, California).

I will write the cities you suggest on the blackboard. Think hard. Try to remember places you have visited or read about. Ready?

Teacher Reference List

Animal Names

Antelope, Calif.
Antelope, Kans.
Beaver, Kans.
Beaverton, Alaska
Big Bear City, Calif.
Big Otter, W. Va.
Bison, Kans.
Bronco, Tex.
Bruin, Ky.
Buckhead, Ga.
Buckskin, Ind.

Buffalo, Idaho, Ky., Tenn.
Bull Shoals, Ark.
Cat Spring, Tex.
Coyote, Calif.
Deerfield, Kans.
Deerfield Beach, Fla.
Deer Trail, Colo.
Elk, Calif.
Elk City, Idaho
Elkhart, Ind.
Elk Horn, Ky.
Fawnskin, Calif.

Teacher Reference List (*cont.*)

Animal Names

Fox, Ark.
Fox Lake, Ill.
Gazelle, Calif.
Gibbonsville, Idaho
Gila Bend, Ariz.
Grizzly Flats, Calif.
Horse Shoe Bend, Idaho
Kodiak, Alaska
Moose Pass, Alaska
Mousie, Ky.
Mule Greek, N. Mex.
Muleshoe, Tex.
N. Wolf Lake, Ill.
Redfox, Ky.
Squirrel, Idaho
Squirrel Is., Me.
Whitehorse, Yukon
Wolf Bayou, Ark.
Wolf Creek, Ky.
Wolflake, Ind.
Wolverine, Ky.

Bird Names

Birdseye, Ind.
Birds Landing, Calif.
Black Hawk, Calif.
Blue Jay, Calif.
Buzzards Bay, Mass.
Chicken, Alaska
Crane, Ind.
Crows Landing, Calif.
Dove Creek, Colo.

Eagle, Alaska, Colo.
Eagle Lake, Fla.
Eagleville, Calif.
Gold Eagle, Ill.
Jay, Fla.
Peacock, Tex.
Pelican, Alaska
Pigeon, W. Va.
Quail, Tex.
Swan Creek, Ill.
Swan Is., Me.
Swan Valley, Ind.
Turkey, Ky., Tex.
Turkey Creek, La.
White Bird, Idaho
Wrens, Ga.

Occupations

Bakersfield, Calif.
Bishop, Tex.
Crook, Colo.
Dyer, Tenn.
Farmer City, Ill.
Farmersville, Calif.
Fishers, Ind.
Goldsmith, Ind.
Hunter, Ark.
Joiner, Ark.
Marshall, Ark.
Mason City, Ill.
Matador, Tex.
Mechanicsburg, Ind.
Millers, Md.

Model, Tenn.
Secretary, Md.
Shepherd, Tex.
Soldier, Ky.
Soldier Pond, Me.
Umpire, Calif.

Names to Wonder About

Accord, Mass.
Ages, Ky.
Best, Tex.
Bim, W. Va.
Bimble, Ky.
Bonnie, Idaho
Book, La.
Broad Bottom, Ky.
Burns, Tenn.
Burnt Prairie, Idaho
Burnt Ranch, Calif.
Bush, La.
Chinese Camp, Calif.
Christmas, Fla.
Coin, Ind.
Cool, Calif.
Cost, Tex.
Cut Off, La.
Cynthiana, Ind.
Dime Box, Tex.
Fallen Leaf, Calif.
Fate, Tex.
Friend, Kans.
Frostproof, Fla.
Gas, Kans.
Goodyears Bar, Calif.

Grand Chain, Ill.
Gravity, Iowa
Gypsy, W. Va.
Happy, Tex.
Hasty, Colo.
Hi Hat, Ky.
Home, Kans.
Honey Creek, Ind.
Hope, Ind.
Humble, Tex.
Joes, Colo.
Ketchum, Idaho
Kettle, Ky.
Kissimmee, Fla.
Little, Ky.
Lone Tree, Iowa
Lost City, W. Va.
Lost Springs, Kans.
Lulu, Fla.
Man, W. Va.
Meddybemps, Me.
Mix, La.
Morning Sun, Iowa
Mystic, Iowa
Nabb, Ind.
Oil City, Pa.
Oolitic, Ind.
Paradise, Utah
Paw Paw, Ky.
Petroleum, Ind., W. Va.
Pie, W. Va.
Pippa Passes, Ky.
Pointblank, Tex.
Raisin, Calif.

Teacher Reference List (*cont.*)

Names to Wonder About

Rising Sun, Ind.	Van, Ark., Tex.
Sac City, Iowa	Vest, Ky.
Sample, Ky.	W. New York, N. J.
Sandwich, Mass.	What Cheer, Iowa
Seven Sisters, Tex.	Wheatfield, Ind.
Shivers, Miss.	Wink, Texas
Shock, W. Va.	Young America, Ind., Minn.
Skygusty, W. Va.	Zag, Ky.
Social Circle, Ga.	
Stamps, Calif.	*Insect Names*
Start, La.	Bee House, Tex.
Street, Md.	Bee Spring, Ky.
Sugar City, Idaho	Beetle, Ky.
Sunny Side, Ga., Tex.	Bumble Bee, Calif.
Sweet, Idaho	Butterfly, Ky.
Sweet Home, Calif.	Honeybee, Ky.
Tilly, Calif.	Kingbee, Ky.

Variation #1: Have players write sentences using some of the strange names. Imagine sentences like these:

1. I'm looking for Lost Spring (Ind.).
2. I haven't been home in Ages (Ky.).
3. I'm in Accord (Mass.) now. I used to live in Hope (Ind.).
4. I've been Home (Kans.), Friend (Kans.). I did not Hi Hat (Ky.) you.
5. I think I'll zig on down to Zag, Kentucky.
6. Where is Mr. Smith? I think you'll find him in Shock (W. Va.).

Variation #2: In hunting strange names, the players will soon find they can easily set up such other classifications as trees, colors, flowers, fruits, first names of men and women, gem stones, faraway places, and duplicates. How many states have a Cleveland, how many a Rome or a Columbus? The only Glenshaw is in Pennsylvania. How many other such cities can be found that have a unique name?

Variation #3:   Have the players write to state capitals or to postmasters of cities and towns whose names intrigue them and ask how the names came about. Read the answers to such inquiries to the group, then post them on the bulletin board. Geography and history can be fascinating fun!

NAME A CITY

Type of Game: Geography   *Grades*:   4 and up
Play Method: Oral individual or team

As an individual game: Begin by naming a city. A volunteer names a city beginning with the last letter of the previously named city. Write the names on the board to avoid duplication.

As a team game: Play as a spell-down type of game. Divide the group into two teams. The first player of team 1 names a city. The first player of team 2 names a city beginning with the last letter of the previously named city. The second player on team 1 continues. If a player misses, a point is scored against his team and play goes to the next player on the opposing team. If a number of players miss in a row, open the game to volunteers from either team. A correct word erases an error point from that player's team score, or gives a credit point to be used against a future error. Play then goes back to the player whose turn was coming up, he takes the city named by the volunteer, and play proceeds.

Reading Directions

This is a city-naming game. I will begin by naming a city. For example, I will say, "New York." Now, who can name a city that begins with the last letter of New York? Suppose the city Kalamazoo were named. Then the next city named must begin with an O. I will write the cities named on the board so that they can't be named again. Ready?

Teacher Reference List (Alphabetical List of Cities)

A Abilene, Acapulco, Akron, Albany, Albuquerque, Alexandria, Algiers, Aliquippa, Allentown, Altoona, Amarillo, Amsterdam, Ankara, Annapolis, Antwerp, Anzio, Arlington, Asheville, Athens, Atlanta, Atlantic City, Augusta, Austin, Aurora.

B Baden-Baden, Baghdad, Bakersfield, Bangkok, Bangor, Barcelona, Bath, Battle Creek, Bayonne, Bayreuth, Beirut, Belfast, Belgrade, Bergen, Berkeley, Berlin, Bethlehem, Beverly Hills, Birmingham, Bismarck, Blackpool, Bloomfield, Bloomington, Bogotá, Bolivar, Bordeaux, Boston, Brasília, Bremen, Bridgeport, Bristol, Brockton.

C Cádiz, Calais, Cairo, Calcutta, Calgary, Cambridge, Canberra, Cannes, Canton, Capetown, Caracas, Cardiff, Carlisle, Carson City, Charleston, Charlotte, Chester, Cheyenne, Chicago, Christchurch, Cincinnati, Cleveland, Clinton, Cologne, Columbia, Columbus, Colorado Springs.

D Dachau, Dakar, Dallas, Damascus, Danville, Danzig, Darwin, Davenport, Dayton, Daytona Beach, Dearborn, Decatur, Delft, Delhi, Delray Beach, Denver, Des Moines, Detroit, Dieppe, Djakarta, Dobbs Ferry, Dover, Dresden, Dublin, Dubuque, Duluth, Dundee, Dunkirk, Durham.

E East Chicago, Easton, East St. Louis, Edinburgh, Edmonton, El Alamein, El Dorado, Elgin, Elizabeth, Elk City, Elkhart, Elmhurst, Elmira, El Paso, Elsinore, Ely, Enid, Erie, Essen, Evanston, Everett,

Elgin, Essex, Eureka, Eureka Springs, Excelsior Springs, Exeter.

F Fairbanks, Fallon, Fall River, Falmouth, Fargo, Farmington, Fayetteville, Fiume, Flagstaff, Flint, Florence, Fort Dodge, Fort Erie, Fort Wayne, Frankfort, Freetown, Fremont, Fresno, Fulton, Furth.

G Galt, Galveston, Gary, Geneva, Ghent, Glasgow, Glendale, Gouda, Granada, Granby, Grand Rapids, Great Falls, Greensboro, Greenwich, Grenoble, Guatemala City.

H Hagerstown, Halifax, Hamburg, Hamilton, Hammond, Hanau, Hangchow, Hannover, Hanoi, Harrisburg, Hartford, Hastings, Havana, Hebron, Helena, Helsinki, High Point, Hoboken, Holyoke, Honolulu, Houston, Hull, Huntington.

I Idaho Falls, Independence, Indianapolis, Inglewood, Interlaken, Interlochen, Inverness, Irvington, Istanbul.

J Jackson, Jefferson City, Jersey City, Jerusalem, Jodhpur, Johnson City, Johnstown, Joliet, Joplin, Juneau.

K Kalamazoo, Kansas City, Karachi, Kenosha, Kiev, Kimberley, Kobe, Kokomo, Krakow, Kuwait, Kyoto.

L La Asuncion, Lafayette, Lagos, Lancaster, Lansing, Larvik, Las Vegas, Lebanon, Leeds, Le Havre, Leipzig, Leopoldville, Lewiston, Los Alamos, Los Angeles, Louisville, Lourdes, Lowell.

M Macon, Malmö, Mandalay, Manila, Mansfield, Mason City, Melbourne, Memphis, Meridian, Mexicali, Miami, Mexico City, Milwaukee, Minneapolis, Monaco, Montclair, Monte Carlo, Montreal.

N Nanking, Nassau, Nazareth, Newark, New Britain, Newburg, Newcastle, New Delhi, New Orleans, Newport News, Newton, New York, Niagara Falls, Nice, Nome, Norfolk, Norwalk, Norwich, Nürnberg.

O Oakland, Oceanside, Odessa, Ogden, Olympia, Omsk, Oneida, Orange, Orlando, Orléans, Osaka, Oshkosh, Oslo, Ottawa.

P Paducah, Pago Pago, Palermo, Panama City, Paris, Parkersburg, Passaic, Paterson, Pawtucket, Peking, Pensacola, Peoria, Perth, Peterborough, Phoenix, Pierre, Pilsen, Pisa, Pittsburgh.

Q Quebec, Queenstown, Quezon City, Quincy.

R Racine, Raleigh, Rangoon, Reading, Regina, Renfrew, Revere, Richmond, Riga, Rio de Janeiro, Rio Grande, Ripley, Riverside, Roanoke, Rochester, Rockford, Rockland, Rome.

S Sacramento, St. Albans, St. John, St. Louis, St. Petersburg, St. Thomas, Salem, Salerno, Salt Lake City, San Bernardino, San Diego, San Fernando, Santa Fe, Sault Sainte Marie, Schenectady, Seattle, Seoul, Sheffield.

T Tacoma, Tallahassee, Tampa, Taunton, Three Rivers, Tijuana, Tipperary, Tokyo, Toledo, Toronto, Tralee, Trenton, Trinidad, Tripoli, Troy, Truro, Tucson, Tulsa.

U Union City, University City, Utica, Utrecht.

V Valencia, Vancouver, Venice, Verdun, Verona, Versailles, Victoria, Vienna, Visby.

W Waco, Waltham, Warren, Warsaw, Washington, Waterbury, Waterford, Waterloo, Waukegan, Wellington, West Orange, Whitehorse, White Plains, Wilkes-Barre, Williamsport, Wilmington, Winchester, Worcester.

X Xanthe, Xochimilco.

Y Yakima, Yalta, Yarmouth, Yokohama, Yonkers, York, Youngstown, Yuba, Yukon.

Z Zachow, Zagreb, Zanesville, Zanzibar, Zenda, Zenith, Zürich.

Variation: Have the players try to name a city for each letter of the alphabet.

PRESIDENTIAL NAME-DOWN

Type of Game: History   Grades: 5 and up
Play Method: Individual or team

As an individual game: The play moves from one player to another player, and so on, in rotation.

As a team game: Play in spell-down style with two teams, play moving from one team to another alternately.

Reading Directions

This is a name-giving game, in which we will use the names of the American Presidents. The first player on team #1 will give the first name of a President. The first player on the second team will name either the middle or last name of that president. He need not give the middle name so long as the last name fits the first name.

Remember, there are several Presidents with the same first name, but if the next player gives a middle name, the next player has only one choice for the last name, the right one.

If a player cannot think of a name, a vote is scored against his team. The play passes to the next player on the other team, who will try to give the right answer.

When one name is completed, the next player begins with the first name of another President. Now, if you are the next player and you think the last player didn't really have a President in mind but just picked a name out of the air, you can challenge him. If he has given a correct name, a vote is scored against your team. But if the challenged player was bluffing, then the vote is registered against his team. The team with the fewer votes wins. Of course, once a President has been named his name cannot be used again in the game. I will keep a check list to make sure that this does not happen. Any questions? Ready?

Teacher Reference List

1. George Washington
2. John Adams
3. Thomas Jefferson

4. James Madison
5. James Monroe
6. John Quincy Adams
7. Andrew Jackson
8. Martin Van Buren
9. William Henry Harrison
10. John Tyler
11. James Knox Polk
12. Zachary Taylor
13. Millard Fillmore
14. Franklin Pierce
15. James Buchanan
16. Abraham Lincoln
17. Andrew Johnson
18. Ulysses Simpson Grant
19. Rutherford Birchard Hayes
20. James Abram Garfield
21. Chester Alan Arthur
22. (Stephen) Grover Cleveland
23. Benjamin Harrison
24. William McKinley
25. Theodore Roosevelt
26. William Howard Taft
27. Woodrow Wilson
28. Warren Gamaliel Harding
29. (John) Calvin Coolidge
30. Herbert Clark Hoover
31. Franklin Delano Roosevelt
32. Harry S. Truman
33. Dwight David Eisenhower
34. John Fitzgerald Kennedy
35. Lyndon Baines Johnson
36. Richard Milhous Nixon

STATES AND CAPITALS

Type of Game: Geography   Grades: 5 and up
Play Method: Oral individual or team game

As an individual game: Call on players in rotation or ask for volunteers.

As a team game: Divide the players into teams by seating rows or divide the group in half, playing one side against the other. Name a state. The player whose turn it is names the capital. Score a point for every correct answer, keeping the team scores on the blackboard. Players may volunteer out of turn to give the nickname of the state, thus adding to their team scores.

Reading Directions

This is a geography game in which we will name the capitals and, if possible, the nicknames of the fifty states. I will name the state, the player whose turn it is will try to name the capital. If he misses, the play goes to the next player on the other team and so on. Each time a correct answer is given a point is scored for that team.

There is a way to get extra points. After a capital has been named, I will ask for volunteers anywhere in the room to name the nickname of that state. A point will be scored for your team if you give the correct answer. Ready?

Teacher Reference List

Name of State	Capital	Nickname
1. Alabama	Montgomery	Cotton State or Heart of Dixie
2. Alaska	Juneau	None
3. Arizona	Phoenix	Grand Canyon State

4. Arkansas	Little Rock	Land of Opportunity
5. California	Sacramento	Golden State
6. Colorado	Denver	Centennial State
7. Connecticut	Hartford	Nutmeg or Constitution State
8. Delaware	Dover	First State or Diamond State
9. Florida	Tallahassee	Sunshine State
10. Georgia	Atlanta	Empire State of the South or Peach State
11. Hawaii	Honolulu	Aloha State
12. Idaho	Boise	Gem State
13. Illinois	Springfield	Land of Lincoln or Prairie State
14. Indiana	Indianapolis	Hoosier State
15. Iowa	Des Moines	Hawkeye State
16. Kansas	Topeka	Sunflower State
17. Kentucky	Frankfort	Blue Grass State
18. Louisiana	Baton Rouge	Pelican State
19. Maine	Augusta	Pine Tree State
20. Maryland	Annapolis	Old Line or Free State
21. Massachusetts	Boston	Old Colony or Bay State
22. Michigan	Lansing	Wolverine State
23. Minnesota	St. Paul	North Star State or Gopher State
24. Mississippi	Jackson	Magnolia State
25. Missouri	Jefferson City	Show Me State
26. Montana	Helena	Treasure State
27. Nebraska	Lincoln	Beef or Cornhusker State
28. Nevada	Carson City	Silver State or Sagebrush State
29. New Hampshire	Concord	Granite State
30. New Jersey	Trenton	Garden State
31. New Mexico	Santa Fe	Land of Enchantment

32. New York	Albany	Empire State
33. North Carolina	Raleigh	Old North or Tarheel State
34. North Dakota	Bismarck	Sioux or Flickertail State
35. Ohio	Columbus	Buckeye State
36. Oklahoma	Oklahoma City	Sooner State
37. Oregon	Salem	Beaver State
38. Pennsylvania	Harrisburg	Keystone State
39. Rhode Island	Providence	Little Rhody
40. South Carolina	Columbia	Palmetto State
41. South Dakota	Pierre	Sunshine or Coyote State
42. Tennessee	Nashville	Volunteer State
43. Texas	Austin	Lone Star State
44. Utah	Salt Lake City	Beehive State
45. Vermont	Montpelier	Green Mountain State
46. Virginia	Richmond	Old Dominion
47. Washington	Olympia	Evergreen State
48. West Virginia	Charleston	Mountain State
49. Wisconsin	Madison	Badger State
50. Wyoming	Cheyenne	Equality State
District of Columbia	Washington, D.C.	None

Variation: With older players, have each player on one team in turn name a state, the next player on the other team naming its capital. Score a point against a team whose player misses. Nicknames should be volunteer information and can be used to erase points. The team with the lowest score wins. Keep a list of states on the blackboard as they are named to avoid duplication and argument.

WORLD GEOGRAPHY NAME-DOWN

Type of Game: Geography   *Grades:* 5 and up
Play Method: Oral team

Divide group into two teams as for a spell-down. The first player names a country, the first player on the second team tries to name the capital. If a player misses, play goes back to the other team. Score a point against the team that misses. If several players miss in a row because the task is too difficult, open the question up to volunteers from any team; a player who comes up with the right answer erases an error point from his team's score. Play then moves back to the next player whose turn was coming up when the volunteer period began.

Reading Directions
This is a world geography game. The first player on the first team names a country, the first player on the second team tries to name the capital. If he succeeds, then the next player on the first team must name a country again. If a player misses, a point is scored against his team and the play goes back to the other team. In other words, play moves back and forth from one team to another.

If several players miss in a row, I will open the game to volunteers. If you can give the right answer, you can erase one of your team's errors. The team with the lowest score wins in this game. One thing is sure—stamp collectors will have an easier time than anybody else in this game!

Note: A comprehensive list is given here, perhaps more comprehensive than needed, but who knows what the modern student will come up with? The list will hopefully help the teacher to give instant answers. The general geographical area is also given in the event the game is played according to the variation (page 68).

Teacher Reference List (Countries and Capitals)

Country	Capital	General Location
Afghanistan	Kabul	South Central Asia
Albania	Tirana	Balkan Peninsula
Algeria	Algiers	North Africa
Andorra	Andorra la Vella	Pyrenees Mountains
Argentina	Buenos Aires	South America
Australia	Canberra	South Pacific
Austria	Vienna	Central Europe
Barbados	Bridgetown	West Indies
Belgium	Brussels	Western Europe
Bhutan	Thimbu	Eastern Himalayas
Bolivia	Sucre	South America
Botswana	Gaberones	South Africa
Brazil	Brasília	South America
Bulgaria	Sofia	Balkan peninsula (on the Black Sea)
Burma	Rangoon	Southeast Asia
Burundi	Bujumbura	East Central Africa
Cambodia	Phnom Penh	Southeast Asia
Canada	Ottawa	North America
Central African Republic	Bangui	Central Africa
Ceylon	Colombo	Indian Ocean
Chad (Republic of)	Fort-Lamy	North Central Africa
Chile	Santiago	South America
China (People's Republic of)	Peking	Eastern Asia
China (Republic of)	Taipei, Taiwan	Eastern Asia

Country	Capital	General Location
Colombia	Bogotá	South America
Congo (Democratic Republic of [the])	Kinshasa	Equatorial Africa
Congo (Republic of [the])	Brazzaville	Equatorial Africa
Costa Rica	San José	Central America
Cuba	Havana	West Indies
Cyprus	Nicosia	Mediterranean Sea
Czechoslovakia	Prague	Central Europe
Dahomey	Porto-Novo	West Africa
Denmark	Copenhagen	Northern Europe
Dominican Republic	Santo Domingo	West Indies
East German Democratic Republic	East Berlin	Central Europe
Ecuador	Quito	South America
El Salvador	San Salvador	Central America
Ethiopia	Addis Ababa	Northeast Africa
Finland	Helsinki	Northern Europe
France	Paris	Western Europe
Gabon Republic	Libreville	West Africa
Gambia	Bathurst	West Africa
Ghana	Accra	West Africa
Greece	Athens	Balkan peninsula
Guatemala	Guatemala City	Central America
Guinea	Conakry	West Africa
Guyana	Georgetown	South America
Haiti	Port-au-Prince	Greater Antilles (West Indies)
Honduras	Tegucigalpa	Central America
Hungary	Budapest	Central Europe
Iceland	Reykjavik	North Atlantic Ocean
India	New Delhi	Southeast Asia

Country	Capital	General Location
Indonesia (Island Republic of)	Djakarta	Southeast Asia
Iran	Tehran	Southwest Asia
Ireland	Dublin	West of Great Britain
Israel	Jerusalem	Middle East
Italy	Rome	Southern Europe
Ivory Coast (Republic of the)	Abidjan	West Africa
Jamaica	Kingston	Caribbean Sea
Japan	Tokyo	North Pacific Ocean
Jordan	Amman and Jerusalem	Middle East
Kenya	Nairobi	East Africa
Korea (Republic of) (South Korea)	Seoul	Northeast Asia
Kuwait	Kuwait City	Northeast Arabia
Laos	Vientiane	Southeast Asia
Lebanon	Beirut	Southwest Asia
Lesotho	Maseru	South Africa
Liberia	Monrovia	West Africa
Libya	Tripoli, Benghazi	North Africa
Liechtenstein	Vaduz	Western Europe
Luxembourg	Luxembourg	Western Europe
Malagasy Republic	Tananarive	West Indian Ocean (off Southeast Africa)
Malawi	Zomba	East Central Africa
Malaysia	Kuala Lumpur, Selangor	Southeast Asia
Maldive Islands	Malé	Indian Ocean
Mali	Bamako	West Africa
Malta	Valletta	Mediterranean Sea
Mauritania (Islamic Republic of)	Nouakchott	West Africa

Country	Capital	General Location
Mexico	Mexico City	Southern North America
Mongolia	Ulan Bator	Northeast Asia
Morocco	Rabat	Northwest Africa
Muscat and Oman	Muscat	Southeast Arabia
Nepal	Katmandu	Himalayas
Netherlands	Amsterdam	Northern Europe
New Zealand	Wellington	South Pacific Ocean
Nicaragua	Managua	Central America
Niger	Niamey	West Africa
Nigeria	Lagos	West Africa
North Korea People's Democratic Republic	Pyongyang	Northeast Asia
Norway	Oslo	Scandinavian peninsula
Pakistan	Islamabad	Southeast Asia
Panama	Panama City	Isthmus of Panama
Paraguay	Asunción	South America
Peru	Lima	South America
Philippines	Quezon City	Western Pacific Ocean
Poland	Warsaw	Central Europe
Portugal	Lisbon	Southwestern Europe
Romania	Bucharest	Southeastern Europe
Rwanda	Kigali	East Central Africa
San Marino	San Marino	Italian peninsula
Saudi Arabia	Riyadh	Arabian peninsula
Senegal	Dakar	West Africa
Sierra Leone	Freetown	West Africa
Singapore	Singapore	Malay peninsula
Somalia	Mogadishu	East Africa
South Africa (Republic of)	Pretoria, Cape Town	South Africa
Spain	Madrid	Western Europe
Sudan	Khartoum	Northeast Africa

Country	Capital	General Location
Sweden	Stockholm	Scandinavian peninsula
Switzerland	Berne	Central Europe
Syria	Damascus	Middle East
Tanzania	Dar es Salaam	East Africa
Thailand (Siam)	Bangkok	Southeast Asia
Togo	Lomé	West Africa
Trinidad and To- bago	Port of Spain	West Indies
Tunisia	Tunis	North Africa
Turkey	Ankara	Asia Minor and South- eastern Europe
Uganda	Kampala	Central Africa
Union of Soviet Socialist Repub- lics	Moscow	Eastern Europe and Northern Asia
United Arab Re- public (Egypt)	Cairo	Northeast Africa
United Kingdom of Great Britain and Northern Ireland	London	Western Europe
Upper Volta	Ouagadougou	West Africa
Uruguay	Montevideo	South America
Venezuela	Caracas	South America
Vietnam (South)	Saigon	Southeast Asia
Vietnam (North)	Hanoi	Southeast Asia
Western Samoa	Apia	South Pacific Ocean
West German Federal Repub- lic	Bonn	Central Europe
Yemen	Saná	Southern Arabian peninsula
Yugoslavia	Belgrade	Southern Europe
Zambia	Lusaka	South Central Africa

Variation: Since some of the capitals are little known and often unpronounceable, allow players to name the general area in which the country is located instead of naming the capital, as South America, Central Africa, South Seas, etc. However, the capitals of countries very much in the news should be named.

III.

SCIENCE *and* NATURE GAMES

ANIMAL ALPHABET

Type of Game: Animal Names   *Grades:* 1 and up
Play Method: Individual oral or written team

As an oral individual game: Call on volunteers to name an animal for a letter of the alphabet. Write the letters on the blackboard in columns. A player may volunteer for any letter not already covered.

As a written team game: Allow five minutes to see how many letters of the alphabet a team can name an animal for.

Reading Directions
I have printed the letters of the alphabet on the blackboard. Let's see if we can name an animal for every letter of the alphabet. Raise your hand if you can name an animal that begins with a particular letter. We will stick to four-legged animals and not include sea animals. It is not necessary that we fill in the letters in alphabetical order, but let's try to find an animal for every letter.

At the end of the game, we will copy the letters we could not find names of animals for. Ask your friends or parents, or visit the library. Then, tomorrow, we will see if we can fill in the blanks.

Teacher Reference List (Animal Alphabet)

A aardvark, agouti, alpaca, anteater, antelope, ape, armadillo

B badger, bat, bear, beaver, bison, bobcat, buffalo, burro, bush baby

C camel, cat, cheetah, chimpanzee, chipmunk, civet, coati, coyote

D dachshund, Dall sheep, Dalmatian, deer, dog, donkey

E eland, elephant, elk, emu

F ferret, field mouse, fitchit, flying lemur, flying squirrel, fox, fox squirrel

G gerbil, gibbon, giraffe, gnu, goat, gopher, gorilla, groundhog, guinea pig

H hamster, hare, hedgehog, hippopotamus, horse

I ibex

J jackal, jackass, jack rabbit, jaguar

K kangaroo, koala, koba, Kodiak bear, kudu

L lemur, lemming, leopard, llama, lynx

M marten, mole, monkey, moose, mouse, mule, muskrat

N Newfoundland dog, nine-banded armadillo, northern flying squirrel, Norway rat

O ocelot, okapi, opossum, otter

P panda, panther, peccary, pig, porcupine, prairie dog, puma

Q quill pig (porcupine)

R rabbit, raccoon, rat, red bat, reindeer, rhinoceros, ringtail

S sheep, shrew, skunk, sloth, squirrel

T tapir, tarsier, tiger

U Utah prairie dog

V vampire bats, varying hare, Virginia deer, vole

W weasel, wolf, wolverine, woodchuck

X

Y yak, yellow-bellied marmot, yuma

Z zebra, zebu

Note: There are no animals for X, but let the players find this out for themselves.

SCIENTIFIC SEARCH

Type of Game: General Science   *Grades*:   4 and up
Play Method: Written team

Divide players into small teams, each with a captain-secretary who records answers and makes his own contributions as well. This game could lead into a lesson in man's dependence upon his environment and the necessity for conservation of natural resources of all kinds.

Reading Directions

This is a science game to test your imagination, your powers of observation, and your knowledge of science. Look around the room, look at your classmates. How many things in the classroom can you find that originally came out of or grew in the ground, or came from animals that lived on the ground or in the sea? It may be something that is part of the room itself. It may be something that someone is wearing. List all the things you can find in five minutes. Not all the things will be in their pure form. They may be combined with another. A pencil of wood that came from a tree contains graphite, a non-metallic mineral that came from the ground. Others may be combinations of things that came from the ground. For example, glass is made of sand, soda or potash, and metallic oxides. Steel is a compound of iron and carbon with varying amounts of other minerals mixed with it depending upon the qualities desired. The addition of nickel and chromium produces hardness and resistance to rusting.

By using your knowledge of the composition of certain materials found in the room, you can come up with a long list in a short time.

What you name may be something you are wearing such as a silver ring with a turquoise setting. Or it might be a woolen sweater made from the wool of a sheep or an Angora goat. Or it might be a cashmere sweater made from the wool from goats of Kashmir or Tibet.

Look hard. Think! There are many objects you can name, some with simple explanations, others with more complicated ones. Talk it over with your teammates. You will be able to help each other.

Note: The reference list is more general than specific but should be helpful. Some of the things listed may not be in the classroom in their original form, but may be combined with one or more of the others. This list supposes that for some players the classroom may be the science room which will contain many of the substances listed either as specimens, parts of a collection, as part of the equipment. Synthetics are included in the list since they are so prevalent.

With younger children the lists compiled will be more specific than general and much simpler in content.

Teacher Reference List

I. Things that Come Out of the Ground
   1. Building Materials (Manufactured from Natural Materials)
      a. cement—an artificial stone made from limestone, shale, gypsum
      b. concrete—made from cement, sand, crushed rock, and water
      c. synthetic materials—vinyl tile, synthetic paints, synthetic rubber tiles (see composition of synthetic materials under that classification)
   2. Building Stones (Natural)
      a. granite
      b. limestone

   c. marble
   d. sandstone
   e. slate
3. Clay
   a. bricks
   b. ceramic vases, dishes
   c. modeling clay
4. Coal
   a. used for heat
   b. part of a rock collection
   c. used in manufacture of synthetics
5. Fossils
   a. as part of a collection
   b. chalk, a fossilized substance
   c. petrified wood gem
   d. limestone often packed with small fossils
6. Gem Stones (Semi-precious and Precious)
   a. as stones set in jewelry
   b. as part of the science room collection

agate	jade	rock crystal
amethyst	jasper	ruby
bloodstone	jet	sapphire
carnelian	lava rock (obsidian)	topaz
diamond	moonstone	tourmaline
emerald	onyx	turquoise
flint	petrified wood	zircon
garnet	quartz	

7. Metallic Minerals
   a. as specimens in a collection
   b. as used in jewelry
   c. as used in building materials
   d. as used in specific objects, as mercury in a thermometer
   e. as used in alloys

aluminum	nickel
chromium	platinum

Teacher Reference List (*cont.*)

copper	silver
gold	tin
iron	uranium
lead	zinc
mercury	

8. Natural Gas
   a. used as fuel, for cooking, in the Bunsen burner, etc.
9. Nonmetallic Minerals
   a. alabaster—for ornaments, bookends, etc.
   b. asbestos—as a fireproofing material in curtains, roofing, insulation
   c. borax—used in making glass, enamels, in chemical experiments, etc.
   d. chalk—as writing material for blackboards (it is interesting to note that chalk is composed of white, soft, shells of small sea animals)
   e. chlorine—used for purification of water and for bleaching purposes
   f. gypsum—used in paints, cement, plaster, tile, and other building materials
   g. graphite—the "lead" in pencils, also used for brushes in motors, and as a lubricant
   h. halite—(common salt) used for seasoning food, in the manufacture of glass, in soapmaking, and in metallurgy
   i. iodine—a by-product of salt, used for medicinal purposes
   j. mica—used for windows in stoves and ovens, and in electronic equipment because of its high electrical resistance
   k. quartz—used in making glass and as a gem
   l. sulphur—used in making matches, in papermaking, and as a source of sulphuric acid
   m. talc—used in cosmetics (face and body powder), as a filler in paint, rubber, and paper

10. Petroleum (Commonly Called Oil)
   a. asphalt type—used in building roads, in the manufacture of building products such as asphalt tiles and roofing compounds
   b. paraffin type—as a fuel for heating, as a fuel for internal combustion engines, in the manufacture of wax for candles, crayons, etc.
11. Sand
   a. in the manufacture of glass, building materials, roads, etc.
12. Water
II. Things that Grow in the Ground
   1. Nonwoody Plants
      a. grains, nuts (peanuts used for many products as well as for eating), root vegetables, ornamental plants, etc.
   2. Trees
      a. wood products used for building products, furniture, toys, pencils, paper-making, etc.
      b. trees whose specific products are rubber, resin, chicle, coffee beans, fruits, nuts, etc.
III. Animals that Grow on the Ground or in the Sea
   1. Animals—used for food, hides for leather, pelts for furs, hair for brushes, bristles for brushes, wool for clothing, wool for felt in erasers, hides, hoofs and bones used in making glue and mucilage
   2. Fish—in aquarium, fish used to make glue, used for food for people and animals
   3. Shells
      a. abalone (a mollusk) used for food and for the shell which is used for jewelry and decorative purposes, for mother-of-pearl buttons and belt buckles
      b. crushed shells used for planting material for flowering bulbs and in aquariums, also for roads
   4. Sponges—the internal skeleton of various marine animals with the ability to absorb water

Teacher Reference List (*cont.*)

IV. Synthetics
  1. Building Materials
      a. synthetic rubber—made from hydrocarbon substances such as petroleum, alcohol, coal tar, natural gas, and acetylene—used for pencil erasers, rubber soles and heels, rubber bands, floor coverings
  2. Clothing
      a. nylon, Orlon, rayon—synthetic fibers made from coal, water, natural gas, oxygen, nitrogen
      b. synthetic gems—made by chemical rather than natural processes used in costume jewelry, as watch jewels, etc.
      c. synthetic leather—a fabric base coated with synthetic material
  3. Miscellaneous
      a. pressure-sensitive materials such as Scotch tape, made of synthetic material coated with adhesives made from gum arabic, a complex organic material from trees

Variation #1:   Give the players words such as ink, paste, pencil. See how many components come from the earth, grew in it or came from animals that lived on the earth or in the sea.

Teacher Reference List

1. Chewing gum—from chicle, the latex of a spodilla tree
2. Glue—made from animal skins, bones, hoofs boiled to a jelly-like substance; also made from fish
3. Ink—from lampblack mixed with glue, tannic acid, or gum, and mixed with aniline dyes for color
4. Envelope—made from paper and treated with an adhesive. Paper is made from wood pulp (some with rag content)
5. Paste—made of a mixture of flour, water, starch, sometimes with alum and resin
6. Shoelace—made from rayon or cotton with a metal tip, sometimes from leather

7. Silk scarf—from a fiber produced by the silkworm in making its cocoon
8. Wooden ruler—made from wood, metal for the strip (usually brass), printed with ink

Variation #2: Give key words such as buttons, belts, jewelry. See how many different materials players can name which these articles can be made from. For example, buttons can be made from leather, bone, shell, wood, synthetics, metal, and glass.

NATURE GOOFS

Type of Game: Nature categories   Grades: 3 and up
Play Method: Oral individual

Call on each player in rotation. As a player fails to name a required word, names an incorrect one, or repeats one already named, write his name on the blackboard and write a G after it. Every time that player misses, an additional letter—O, O, F— is added. When he becomes a full GOOF he is out of the game. He can however, erase a letter by volunteering a word during the volunteer periods in the game.

Reading Directions

In this game we are going to name as many words in a certain nature category or group as we can. For example, I might give the classification trees. Each player in turn must name a kind of tree. When a player cannot do so, he becomes a fourth of a GOOF. For every miss a player makes, a letter of the word GOOF is written after his name. A full GOOF is out of the game. But a player can erase a part of a GOOF by volunteering a correct word when one is called for. For example, if several players in a row miss, I will ask for volunteers out of turn. If you can give a correct word at that time, you can erase one of the letters. In that way you may be able to keep yourself from being eliminated from the game.

After the volunteer period, I will give a new classification such as birds, snakes, animals, or fish. We will begin again with the player whose turn was coming up. One more thing—if you can volunteer an answer but don't have a GOOF letter to erase, you can have a credit point to use in case you miss on your next time around. Just like money in the bank!

Let's try to keep the game moving as fast as possible. Ready?

Note: With younger children, change the classification often.

Teacher Reference List

Trees	
acacia	sycamore
aspen	tulip poplar
beech	willow
black cherry	
black walnut	Birds
buckeye	blue jay
catalpa	buzzard
cottonwood	cardinal
cypress	dove
fir	duck
ginkgo	eagle
hemlock	falcon
locust	flamingo
magnolia	flicker
maple	flycatcher
mulberry	goldfinch
oak	grackle
pecan	gull
pignut hickory	hawk
pine	heron
redwood	hummingbird
sassafras	junco
spruce	lark
sweet gum	loon
	owl

pigeon
purple martin
redwing blackbird
robin
sparrow
starling

Fish

bass
bonito
catfish
dogfish
flounder
guppy
haddock
hake
halibut
herring
lamprey
marlin
minnow
perch
pickerel
rainbow trout
salmon
shad
sturgeon
sunfish
tiger fish
trout
tuna
walleye

Mammals

anteater
antelope
ape

armadillo
buffalo
bull
cat
chimpanzee
civet
cow
deer
dog
dolphin
koala
kudu
leopard
lion
manatee
monkey
otter
platypus
seal
sheep
tiger
walrus
whale
zebu

Snakes

adder
boa
bull snake
chicken snake
cobra
copperhead
diamondback
grass snake
king snake
milk snake
moccasin

Teacher Reference List (*cont.*)

Snakes
python
rattler
sidewinder
viper
worm snake

Cultivated Flowers
ageratum
amaryllis
aster
azalea
begonia
calendula
Canterbury bell
crocus
daffodil
daisy
forget-me-not
geranium
hibiscus
hollyhock
hyacinth
iris
Johnny-jump-up
larkspur
lavender
marigold
mock orange
morning glory
peony
pink
poppy
rose
tulip

Wildflowers
adder's-tongue
aster
black-eyed Susan
bloodroot
buttercup
chickweed
clover
coneflower
cowslip
dandelion
day lily
Dutchman's-breeches
Indian paintbrush
lady's slipper
mallow
mayapple
Queen Anne's lace
self-heal
skunkweed
spring beauty
sticktight
thistle
touch-me-not
violet
wintergreen
yarrow

Variation: Play as a spell-down type of game and organize two teams. The first player names the category and gives an example. The second player continues in that category. After a certain number of examples, the next player names a new category and gives an example. Write the words used on the blackboard to avoid duplication. Score a point for each correct word. With younger children, limit the play in each category to six examples. With older players, allow each classification to run for ten or twelve examples before the change.

IV.

WORD GAMES

How many words could we figure are heard or read by the average individual in his lifetime? The number would surely be astronomical. But without a well-developed sense of awareness, how much of the information with which the individual is bombarded sinks in? How much of it is ignored? How much of it is understood? Awareness—that quality of alertness or sensitivity—is vital to the acquisition of knowledge through the senses. Before we can interpret what we see, hear, feel, taste, or smell, it is first necessary that we be aware. To look at something is not necessarily to see it; to be exposed to sound does not mean that we consciously hear it.

Awareness is not an inherited trait; it is a developed skill. Without it we are less than we can be. Only when we possess it can we become wholly developed, completely functioning human beings.

Words are excellent tools in the development of awareness, and games that challenge our senses and strain our vocabularies help to develop awareness through play methods. Through them we learn that it is not enough to see something, in all the meanings of the word, but that we must be able to communicate what we have seen to another. How frustrating it is to become aware of beauty, injustice, ugliness, evil, or inspiration, and not be able to communicate that awareness to another. We have the words with which to communicate in our language, but we are not born with a vocabulary. This we must acquire, and to do so we need to be acquainted with the resources that help us to find the right words for the right occasions. For this reason we have made some games dictionary hunts. Hopefully, the dictionary will become a welcome piece of game equipment, a fun thing to use as well as a valuable aid.

Awareness, communication, involvement—these three words are vital to the preservation of our civilization. Word games can play an important role in education for living, but whether skill with words is developed through games that make words fun to use, or through the formal methods of classroom teaching, is not important. What matters is that each individual develops awareness and the ability to communicate with his fellow man to the best of his ability. Only then will what he becomes be the best he can be. Only then can he be a functioning member of the community of the world.

Spelling Games

CHANGE LETTERS—CHANGE WORDS

Type of Game: Word (spelling)   *Grades:* 3 and up
Play Method: Individual written

Reading Directions
In this game we will take one word and try to change it into another by changing only one letter at a time. The trick is that each time you change a letter you must make a new word. Let's try, for example, to change a cat into a dog. We will change only

one letter at a time, and each time we will make a new word. Watch.

c-a-t, c-o-t, d-o-t, d-o-g

In three changes we have changed *cat* to *dog*. That is part of the game, too, to see how few steps are needed to complete the change.

Let's work out one example together so we are all sure how the game works. Then each of you will try on your own. Let's try to change *east* to *west*.

e-a-s-t, f-a-s-t, f-e-s-t, w-e-s-t

You may use your dictionaries if you think that will help you. Ready?

Teacher Reference List

1. bus, but, cut, cur, car
2. boy, bay, ban, man
3. cold, cord, word, ward, warm
4. head, heed, feed, feet
5. tip, top, toe
6. lead, load, goad, gold
7. town, tows, tots, pots, pits, pity, city
8. nose, hose, host, most, moss, toss, toes
9. beer, bear, beat, bent, lent, lint, line, wine
10. ring, rang, hang, hand
11. shoe, shot, soot, toot, took, tock, sock
12. bead, bend, bind, bird
13. rain, pain, pair, fair
14. seed, feed, fled, flee, free, tree
15. run, ran, rat, sat, sit
16. lost, lose, hose, home
17. work, pork, pore, lore, love, live
18. sick, silk, sill, will, well

19. try, toy, ton, tin, win
20. meat, seat, slat, slaw, slew, stew
21. poor, moor, mood, good
22. work, pork, perk, pert, pest, rest
23. good, food, foot, loot, lost, lest, best
24. walk, wall, tall, tale, tile, tide, ride
25. hard, hart, mart, mast, most, lost, loft, soft
26. some, sore, more, mare, mane, many

LETTER FUN

Type of Game: Word   Grades: 3 and up
Play Method: Oral or written, individual or team

As an oral individual game: Pose the problem and have the players volunteer answers, which are then written on the blackboard.

As a written individual game: Same as above, except that each player writes his list. After the time limit is up, call on each player in turn to name a word on his list. Write these on the board. When no new word can be supplied from the players' lists, the player with the longest correct lists of words wins.

As a team game: Divide the group into teams, each with a secretary-captain. The captain writes the words suggested by his teammates, adding his own, of course. At the end of the time limit, ask for words from each team captain in turn, writing the words on the blackboard. The team with the longest list of correct words wins.

Reading Directions
If you were to look in the dictionary, which letters of the alphabet have the fewest pages? X? Z? Q? Y? X has the fewest words of all, then come Z, Y, and Q in that order.

Let's see how many words we can name that begin with X, Z, Q, and Y. X words will count 25 points, Z words 20 points, Y words 10 points, and Q words 5 points. At the end of five minutes we will take time to check (*individual* or *team*) lists. Ready?

Teacher Reference Lists

Note: Lists are not complete, of course, but in most lists even younger children could find words they would know.

X		Y	
xenon	zinc		yearly
xenophobia	zing	yacht	yearn
Xerxes	zinnia	yah	yeast
Xmas	Zion	yahoo	yegg
x-ray	Zionist	yak	yell
xylophone	zip	yam	yellow
	zipper	yammer	yelp
	zircon	Yangtze	yen
Z	zither	yank	yeoman
Zachariah	zodiac	Yankee	yes
zany	zoo	yap	yet
zeal	zone	yard	yew
zebra	zoologic	yardage	Yiddish
zealous	zoology	yardstick	yield
zebrawood	zoom	yarn	yip
Zeeland	zoot suit	yarrow	yipe
zenith	Zoroaster	yaw	yodel
zephyr	zucchini	yawl	yoga
zero	Zulu	yawn	yoke
zest	Zuñi	ye	yokel
zestful	zwieback	yea	yolk
Zeus		year	yonder
zigzag		yearbook	yore
zillion		yearling	you

young	quadruplet	quarterly	quiet
yours	quagmire	quartet	quill
yourself	quahog	quartz	quilt
youth	quail	quash	quinine
yowl	quaint	quaver	quintet
yoyo	quake	quay	quintuplets
yucca	Quaker	queasy	quire
Yugoslavia	quaking	Quebec	quite
Yukon	qualification	queen	quits
yule	qualify	queer	quitter
	qualm	quench	quiz
Q	quandary	query	quoit
quack	quantity	quest	quorum
quadrangle	quarantine	question	quota
quadrant	quarrel	queue	quote
quadrille	quarry	quick	
quadruped	quart	quicken	
quadruple	quarter	quicksilver	

ALPHABET OBJECT HUNT

Type of Game: Word   Grades: 3 and up
Play Method: Oral individual or written team

As an oral individual game: For younger children, to whom
spelling might be a problem, play this game as an oral one.
Write the letters of the alphabet on the board, one under the
other, and have the children volunteer objects that begin with a
particular letter of the alphabet, or persons whose first names
begin with a certain letter. Try to fill in all the letters first
before going for second examples of each letter.

As a written team: With older children, divide the group into
teams, each with a secretary-captain who writes the letters of

the alphabet on a sheet of paper. He then records the suggestions of his teammates, and makes his contributions as well. In scoring, give five points for the first correct word for each letter. If time has permitted giving more than one example for some letters, score an extra point for these words. But it is the first correct word following each letter that scores five points. Thus a team that fills in a word after each letter can make a higher score than a team that might have ten words for only three or four letters.

Reading Directions

This is an alphabetical treasure hunt. We will take all the letters of the alphabet and try to find some thing or a person in this room whose name begins with a particular letter of the alphabet. Let's see how many letters of the alphabet we can find an object or a person for. Some letters will be easier than others, but let's try to fill in the entire alphabet before we try to find second and third examples for the easier letters.

We will score five points for each letter of the alphabet for which you have a correct word. Any extra words you might have for any letter will score one point each. Try to get at least one word for each letter. You can get a larger score that way than if you find several words for only a few different letters. Ready?

Teacher Reference List

Note: This list can only surmise as to the contents of a room, but may still be helpful. Names of players will fill in many an empty space.

A atlas, attendance book, aunt (a child who is one)
B blackboard, blotter, book, book ends, boys, blue (color) broom, brown (color) brush

C   calendar, ceiling, chair, chalk, clock, corkboard, corner, crayons
D   date (on calendar), design, desk, dictionary, door, dustpan
E   easel, electric light, eraser, eyeglasses
F   felt marker, file, fixture, flag, floor, frame, front
G   girls, glass, glove, glue, grammar book, green (color)
H   hair, hair ribbon, handle, hanger, heat, heel, hinge, hole, hook
I   indelible pencil, ink, ink eraser, insect, intercom, iron
J   jamb (window or door), jar, joint
K   kerchief, key, knife, knob (door), knot
L   lamp, light, light switch, lock, locket
M   magazine, magnifying glass, map, marker, metal object
N   nail, needle, number (on calendar or clock), nut (metal)
O   odds (and ends), oil can, oneself, opening, orange (color), Orlon
    (clothing), outlet
P   paper, pen, pencil, pencil sharpener, picture, plants, players,
    pupils
Q   quadrangle, quarter, quicksilver (in thermometer), quotation
R   radiator, radio, rag, reader, rear, red (color), register, ring, ruler
S   scissors, seats, shoe sole, sill, sink, stapler, steel
T   teacher, thermometer, thermostat, thumbtack, trousers
U   umbrella, uncle (a child who is one), unit
V   vase, ventilator, vial, view, vine
W   wall, wand, wastebasket, watch, water, window, wire, wood
Y   yardstick, yarn, yellow (color), you, youths
Z   zipper

PLURAL PUZZLERS

Type of Game: Word   Grades: 4 and up
Play Method: Written individual or team

There are some words whose plural is spelled the same as the singular form. To use such words in a game, write a list of them on the blackboard and then ask players to write the plurals of each. Or ask the players, as individuals or teams, to compile a list of words that meet the necessary qualifications. The method used depends upon the age of the group.

Reading Directions

Words have a way of being tricky. The puzzlers we are playing with are those words which are spelled the same both in the singular and plural forms. An example of this type of word is *sheep*. How many such words can you name in five minutes? At the end of the time period I will call on each player to give one word. Let's see how many words we will have on our list.

Teacher Reference List

alms	gallows	pants
barracks	glasses	pliers
blues (music)	gross	salmon
cards (as game)	Iroquois	scissors
Chinese	Japanese	shears
clippers	lodgings	sheep
coveralls	means	Swiss
deer	moose	tongs
forceps	overalls	trousers

SPELL-A-WORD RELAY

Type of Game: Active spelling   *Grades:* 1 and up
Play Method: Two-team relay

For this game, two sets of alphabet cards large enough to be seen across the room are needed. Letters should be printed on cards of two different colors or with two different-colored felt pens so that the teams can distinguish their cards easily.

Divide the group into two teams. (It is not necessary to have teams of equal numbers in this game.) Line the teams up several yards back from a table on which the two sets of alphabet cards have been placed. The cards need not be in alphabetical order.

This is an active, exciting, and often noisy game. Forewarned is forearmed!

Note: Since the words to be spelled are those that use any letter of the alphabet only once, a ready reference list is included.

Reading Directions

This is a spelling relay. I will tell you first how many letters are in the word to be spelled. For example, if I say that the word has five letters in it, the first five players on each team get ready to move. Then, when I tell you the word, the first five players on each team go to the table, find the right letters to spell the word, and then line up facing their team. The first team to spell the word correctly gets a point. As soon as the point is scored, these players put their cards back on the table and move to the end of their team line. The next players then get ready to run up and spell the next word.

I will give you a hint to make the game easier for you. If the first player in line looks for the first letter of the word, and the second player the next letter, and so on, then you will not all be looking for the same letter. Each of you will look for a particular letter and line up in the proper place after you find it.

Note: With younger children, play as above with one exception. You might spell the word for the players. They still must find the right letter and take the correct place in line.

Teacher Reference List

Four-letter words

game	many	lead	team	sing	flat
four	song	cats	time	dogs	oval

Teacher Reference List (*cont.*)

Four-letter words

head	rain	toes	cows	body	glad
warn	blue	wilt	pink	lose	
such	word	name	card	felt	
hurt	than	this	what	boys	
fork	desk	auto	life	swim	

Five-letter words

games	snake	ladle	learn	barks	beach
first	words	guard	knife	write	birds
laugh	short	white	slink	ruler	ready
bread	fails	foxes	brown	round	reads
girls	great	times	among	black	rough
label	teach	sadly	candy	loser	quick

Six-letter words

friend	single	mailer	scored	bakers
saying	pencil	triple	banker	flower
square	writes	orange	crying	basket
bowler	player	riders	writer	county
yearns	finder	second	points	double

Variation #1: Sometimes, instead of naming the word to be spelled, give a classification such as color, trees, proper names, or animals. The players must then decide among themselves what word they are going to spell.

Variation #2: Double certain vowels or consonants in the alphabet cards. This will make possible a larger variety of words. Doubling the e and o only will make many more words possible. Doubling the s, t, f, and r will also add to the variety and difficulty of words to be spelled.

SPELLING BASEBALL GAME

Type of Game: Spelling   Grades: 3 and up
Play Method: Oral team

This is a combination spelling and baseball game, so it is necessary that the children understand the game of baseball to play it. Draw a baseball diamond on the blackboard and, below it, a score card showing five innings. Divide the group into two teams. One team is "at bat," the second is "in the field." Using a graded spelling list, give a word to the first player, who will attempt to spell it. If he spells it correctly, he scores a hit and goes to first base. (The player stays in his place, but a marker is placed on first base on the diagram.) A misspelled word is an out, but only if the team in the field recognizes it as misspelled. If no protest is made by the fielding team, the player goes to first on an error, advancing the first "runner" to second. At the end of three outs (recognized misspelled words), the teams change sides, and the runs scored in that inning are shown on the score card. At the end of three or five innings, depending upon how much time you have, the winner is declared.

Note: A flannel board will work better than the blackboard to keep "runners" on base. But if you have no flannel board, make cardboard markers and place a ring of masking or Scotch tape on the back of each one and stick it to the blackboard. Move it around as necessary.

Reading Directions

This is a spelling game played like baseball. We have a team at bat and one in the field. I will pitch a word to the first player at bat. He will spell it. If he spells it correctly it is a hit, and I will put a marker at first base. If a batter misspells a word and the team at field knows he has spelled it incorrectly, the batter is out. But if the fielding team does not recognize the word as incorrectly spelled, the batter goes to first on an error. Every player has to be on his toes.

We will play three or five innings, depending upon how fast the game moves along. The team with the bigger score wins, just as in baseball. I will keep track of the errors, too, so you will know how many errors each team scored. Ready?

Variation: Play in the same manner as described in the rules, but place three chairs at the front of the room. These are designated as first, second, and third base. As a player makes a "hit," he moves from his seat to first base. He advances as his teammates also make "hits." A runner moves from third base to his own seat, scoring a run.

SPORTS EXPRESSIONS

Type of Game: Word   Grades: 4 and up
Play Method: Individual oral or written team

As an individual oral game: Present the challenge, calling on players to volunteer expressions.

As a written team game: Players are divided into teams, each with a secretary-captain who records his teammates' suggestions and makes his own contributions as well. At the end of a limited time period, captains are called on to read their lists. The longest list of suitable expressions wins.

Reading Directions

We use many expressions in everyday speech that are really sports expressions, but we are not necessarily discussing sports at that moment. For example, we might say of someone who is having a difficult time doing something: "He can't get to first base." Or about someone whom we think is not particularly likable: "He's a foul ball." These, of course, are baseball expressions. We have others that come from other sports.

Let's see how many sports-type expressions like the examples I have mentioned we can think of. The best way to get started in your thinking is to take one particular sport, such as baseball. Think of some of the parts of the game and the expressions will come.

Teacher Reference List (Sports Expressions)

1. Two strikes against him
2. To be in the swim
3. Right down my alley
4. Paddle your own canoe
5. To get one's oar in
6. Left at the post
7. Out of bounds
8. Go roll a hoop
9. Go fly a kite
10. To be on the ball
11. Start the ball rolling
12. Get in there and pitch
13. Throw in the towel
14. Throw someone for a loss
15. Knock someone for a goal
16. To be a dead ringer for someone
17. To get a stranglehold on someone
18. To have an ace in the hole
19. Play dirty pool
20. Behind the eight ball
21. High stepper
22. To throw someone a curve
23. To do something that's "not cricket"

Note: Suggest that the players try this game out on their friends and family to see if they can come up with expressions other than those compiled during the playing of the game.

Variation #1: Play using animal-oriented terms.

Teacher Reference List (Animal Expressions)

1. Snake in the grass
2. To be catty
3. To shoot the bull
4. A bird in hand
5. Mad as a hornet
6. Crazy like a fox
7. Stubborn as a mule, or mulish
8. Butterflies in the stomach
9. To be a sucker
10. To see pink elephants
11. To be a wolf
12. To monkey around
13. Sheep or calf eyes
14. Strong as an ox
15. Beetle-browed
16. Dirty as a pig
17. Bats in his belfry
18. He's a worm
19. Cheerful as a cricket
20. Eager beaver

Variation #2: Expressions that have familiar household items in them are also fun to play with. A reference list follows.

Teacher Reference List (Household Expressions)

1. That's cooking with gas
2. Cooking on the front burner
3. Out of the frying pan into the fire

4. Calling the kettle black
5. Sharp as a tack
6. Hit the nail on the head
7. Soft soap
8. To needle someone
9. Treat someone like a doormat
10. Born with a silver spoon in her mouth
11. To be a stoolie
12. Little pitchers have big ears
13. To have enough on one's plate (a lot of trouble)
14. She's quite a dish
15. A new broom sweeps clean
16. Comfortable as an old shoe
17. Smokes like a chimney
18. Crooked as a corkscrew
19. To pan someone
20. To cut a rug

Note: Challenge the players to find other classifications of expressions. Some examples are birds (birds of a feather or bird brain); food (peaches and cream complexion, butter and egg man); sewing (the seamy side and skirting an issue); parts of the body (caught flat-footed and chip on the shoulder).

SPELLING RELAY

Type of Game: Written spelling relay   Grades: 3 and up
Play Method: Team

Divide the players into teams, each with a player-captain. Each player has a piece of paper with his name at the top and a pencil.

Reading Directions

This is a spelling game, but it is spelling with a trick to it. I will tell you the number of letters you must use and what the first and last letters must be. You must fill in the middle letters to make a word. For example, I might say write a four-letter word beginning with b and ending with d. You might write bird, bead, or band. Don't look to see what your teammate is writing. Find your own word. As soon as you have written one, pass your paper to your captain. When the captain has all the papers from his team, he stands.

When all the captains are up, the captain of the first team will read and spell all the words his team has written. For each different word correctly spelled, the team scores one point. If you have all written the same word, your team would score only one point.

When we have heard the words from all the teams, the captains will pass the papers back to their teammates, and I will give you the next word to work on.

Remember each different word scores a point, so try to find your own word. As a hint to make it easier for you, try putting a vowel as the second letter. The rest of the word should come easily.

Teacher Reference List

Four-letter words

1. b–d bald, band, bead, bend, bind, bled, bold, brad, bred
2. r–t rant, rapt, rent, rest, rift, riot, rout, runt, rust
3. t–l tail, tall, teal, tell, till, toll, tool
4. c–t cant, cart, cast, cent, chat, chit, clot, coat, colt, coot, cult, curt
5. d–t daft, dart, debt, deft, dent, diet, dirt, dolt, duct, duet, dust
6. w–t waft, wait, want, wart, weft, welt, went, wept, west, whet, wilt, wont, wort, writ

7. g–l   gall, gill, girl, goal, gull
8. h–e   hare, hate, have, haze, here, hide, hike, hire, hive, hole, home, hone, hope, hose, huge
9. l–e   lace, lake, lame, lane, late, life, like, line, live, lode, lone, lope, lore, lose, love, lube, lure, lute, lyre
10. m–t   malt, mart, mast, meat, meet, melt, mist, mint, moat, most, must
11. r–e   race, rage, rake, rape, rare, rate, rave, raze, rice, ride, rife, rile, ripe, rise, rite, rode, role, rope, rose, rote, rove, rule, ruse
12. s–e   safe, sage, sake, sale, same, sane, save, sire, site, sole, some, sure
13. m–e   mace, made, make, male, mane, mare, mate, maze, mere, mete, mice, mile, mire, mite, mode, mole, mope, more, move, mule, muse, mute
14. p–l   pail, pall, peal, peel, pill, pool, pull
15. r–t   raft, rant, rapt, rust, rent, rest, riot, root, runt

Five-letter words

1. t–s   tales, taxes, toots, tears, tends, terms, tests, tides, times, tires, tolls, tomes, trays, trees, tubes, tunes, types
2. t–e   trace, trade, tense, terse, theme, there, these, those, three, thyme, tripe, twice
3. c–e   cable, cadge, calve, carve, caste, chase, chose, coupe, crane, crepe, crone
4. s–e   sense, shake, shape, share, shave, snake, snare, skate, slate, spade, stage, stake, stale, stare, state, stove, style
5. g–e   glade, glaze, glide, globe, glove, gouge, grace, grade, grape, graze, gripe
6. l–e   ladle, lance, lapse, large, lathe, leave, loose, louse
7. w–e   weave, whale, where, while, white, whole
8. p–e   paste, peace, phase, phone, pique, place, plane, plate, prime, prose, purse
9. e–r   eager, eater, edger
10. h–y   hairy, handy, heady, hilly, hoary, hobby, holly

11. f—e   false, farce, fence, flake, flame, flare, flume, force, forge, frame, fuzee

12. r—r   racer, radar, raker, rarer, rater, razer, razor, ricer, rider, rigor, ruler

13. b—e   barge, bilge, blade, blame, blare, blaze, brave, brake, bulge

14. d—y   daily, daisy, dandy, decay, delay, dirty, dolly, dopey, dully

15. g—s   gates, genes, glass, glens, gloss, goats, grass, gross

Variation #1: Play as a dictionary treasure hunt, either team or individual. As a team game, suggest that each team member look under a different vowel. For example, if the letters were w--e, one player would look under wa, another we, a third under wi, etc. As the players search their dictionaries, they will find other words whose second letter may be a consonant; this is especially true of five-letter words. When dictionaries are used, the teams should find five or ten words for each letter combination and should be ready to define "new" words as well.

Variation #2: When playing with young children, the game is easier if the demand is for three- or four-letter words without beginning or ending letter restrictions.

Variation #3: Ask for five-, six-, or seven-letter words, giving only the first letter. This is still challenging, but a little easier.

THIRD OF A "GHOST"

Type of game: Spelling   *Grades*: 3 and up
Play Method: Oral individual

Play goes from one player to the next in rotation.

Reading Directions

This is a spelling game. The first player names a letter, any letter, to begin a word. The next player adds a letter but must also have a word in mind that is spelled in that way. For example, the first player says *b*, the second player, with the word *brave* in mind, adds an *r*. The third player adds the letter *u*, with the word *brunt* in mind. The object of the game is to add a letter without finishing a word. If a player cannot think of a word with the letters already named he can challenge the last player to name his word. If that player had a real word in mind and names it, the challenging player scores a miss and is a third of a GHOST. A new word is then begun by the next player. If, however, the challenged player did not have a word in mind, then the challenged player scores an error and *he* becomes a third of a GHOST. A player who becomes a full ghost is eliminated from the game. I will keep score on the blackboard as a player becomes a part of a ghost. When a player has three thirds written after his name, he is eliminated from the game.

Now, if you are alert, there are ways of not ending a word. For example, the word spelled so far may be *b-r-a-v*. The next player can avoid ending it by adding an *i* so that the word would be *braving* instead of *brave*.

You not only have to be careful which letter you add so that you don't end a word you might have in mind, but you must be careful that in thinking of one word you have overlooked another word hiding in that word. Take, for example, the letters *r-u*. You may have the word *runt* in mind, but in adding an *n* you have completed the word *run*, and there you are—a third of a GHOST.

I think you'll find that this is a good game to play when you are bored with riding in the school bus or on a long trip or when you have to sit and wait for something. It can be played with two players as well as a large number.

Ready? Let's see if we can move quickly now.

Variation: Rule out three-letter words to help eliminate the possibility of ending a word inadvertently.

THIRD OF AN "UGH"

Type of Game: Spelling   *Grades:* 4 and up
Play Method: Oral individual

Play goes from one player to another in rotation.

Reading Directions

This is a spelling game. The first player names the two letters that begin a word he has in mind. The next player, not knowing the word the first player has in mind, must add two more letters, but he too must have a word in mind that is spelled in that manner. Each player in turn must add two letters. The trick is to add letters without finishing a word. The player who finishes a word is a third of an UGH. When a player becomes a full UGH, he drops out of the game. I will keep score on the blackboard, writing a letter after a player's name after each miss.

Remember, you cannot add just any two letters, you must have a word in mind that is spelled in the manner. You can be challenged by the next player if he thinks you are faking. If you are challenged and don't have a legitimate word, you become a third of an UGH. If, however, you can name a word, then the challenger becomes a third of an UGH.

The trick is to add two letters and not complete a word without meaning to, since one word often hides in another. For example, suppose the letters so far are *p-r* and you have the word *prophet* in mind. You add *o-p*. In spelling *prop* you have finished a word, and there you are, a third of an UGH!

There is another trick to remember in this game. Sometimes by changing a word to an *i-n-g* ending, you can force the next player to end it. For example, suppose it is your turn and the letters so far are *p-a-r-a*. Now, if you add *d-e* you have finished the word *parade*. But if you change the word from *parade* to *parading*, then you can add a *d-i*, and the next person is left to finish the word with *n-g*, if he cannot think of another word.

To make the game easier, we will not insist that the challenged words be six-, eight- or ten-letter words. A word of an uneven number of letters will be accepted. This means that sometimes the player stuck with ending the word will be able to add only one letter.

Variation #1: When playing with older players, rule out four-letter words as complete words to eliminate a player inadvertently ending a word on a second play.

Variation #2: For older players, insist the words spelled must be six-, eight- or ten-letter words. In other words, the player forced to finish a word must be able to add two letters. If he can add only one letter, he can challenge the previous player, putting the penalty on him.

Variation #3: Play in the same manner, using full syllables instead of two letters. In this game, a player might add from one to four letters at a time, depending upon the word being spelled.

Dictionary Hunts

A dictionary is a familiar part of a classroom. It is recognized as an important resource and reference book. It can also become known as a fun book to use in word games.

If playing with words seems more fun than studying words, don't be alarmed—the end result is the same. Everyone knows more at the end of the game than he did at the beginning. Most important, we learn that words can be fun. And when such experiences are enjoyable, we tend to repeat them, making them a part of our life pattern, helping to establish good habits of fun.

In dictionary hunts, a player often finds more than he is looking for at the moment. He learns many things about his dictionary and comes to look upon it as a friendly necessity in his life.

Hopefully, with encouragement from the teacher, the players will "take" a game home with them and bring back ideas they have discovered through private research or been given by more knowledgeable friends and family members.

DOUBLED-VOWEL DICTIONARY HUNT

Type of Game: Word   *Grades*: 4 and up
Play Method: Written individual or team

As an individual game: Players compile words, during a limited time, using dictionaries. Each must be able to locate geographical names or define strange words. At the end of the time period, teacher asks players in turn for words, writing them on the blackboard to avoid duplications. The player with the longest correct list wins.

As a team game: Divide the group into teams, each of which has a secretary-captain who records his teammates' suggestions and adds his own contributions as well. At the end of the time period, the teacher calls on each captain in turn for a word with a doubled a in it. On the second round, the doubled e words are called for, etc. The doubled *i* and doubled *u* words are the most difficult, of course.

Reading Directions

We know the vowels *a, e, i, o,* and *u.* All of these appear in words in doubled fashion, some more often than others. For example, it is easy to find words with a doubled *e* or a doubled *o* in them, but the ones with a doubled *a, i,* and *u* are extremely difficult to find. The doubled letters may come at the beginning, within, or at the end of the word. Proper names are permissible. Examples of the kinds of words we are looking for are *beet, moon.* I will not give you many examples of the doubled *a, i,* or *u.* You will have to find them for yourselves.

List the vowels across the top of the page and then write your words under the proper letters. Start with A section in your dictionary, find your doubled *a* words, and then try to fill in some of the easy combinations, such as the *ee* and *oo* words. Then try to find the *ii* and the *uu* words. Good hunting! Ready?

Teacher Reference List

aa	*ee*	*ii*	*oo*	*uu*
aardvark	been	genii	bamboo	duumvir (one
aardwolf	beer	Hawaii	bassoon	of two
Aaron	beet	Hawaiian	bazooka	rulers)
baa	deep	Hiiumaa	boohoo	duumvirate
Baal	feel	radii	boom	(A two-man
bazaar	free	skiing	gloom	rule)
Canaan	geese		good	ignis fatuus
Canaanite	jubilee		hooligan	(will-o'-the-
Hiiumaa (Estonian	keel		hooray	wisp)
island)	keep		lagoon	vacuum
Kaaba (sacred	reel		moon	
Moslem shrine)	steel		room	
			toot	

Note: Suggest that players challenge friends and family to add
to this list, especially in the *ii* and *uu* lists.

Variation: By the same method, try to find words which end
in doubled vowels. There are none with a doubled u.

Teacher Reference List

aa	ee	ii	oo	uu
Baa	agree	genii	bamboo	(none)
Hiiumaa	bee	Hawaii	boo	
(Estonian island)	dungaree	radii	boohoo	
	flee		coo	
	free		igloo	
	gee		kangaroo	
	jubilee		taboo	
	knee		tattoo	
	levee		too	
	lichee		voodoo	
	manatee		woo	
	negligee		yahoo	
	rupee			
	see			
	tee			
	thee			
	wee			

Note: Suggest to players that they challenge their friends and
families to add to this list.

DICTIONARY VOWEL HUNT

Type of Game: Word   Grades: 4 through 8
Play Method: Oral individual or written team

As an oral individual game: Within a time limit, the players search the dictionary for the type of words required, making a written list. At the end of the time period, the teacher asks each child in turn to give a word and spell it while the teacher writes it on the blackboard. Definitions may be demanded for strange words.

As a written team game: The group is divided into teams, each with a captain-secretary who records suggestions from his team-mates, adding his own contributions as well. At the end of the time limit, the teacher calls on each team in turn, asking for one word at a time.

Reading Directions

We all know the five vowels, a, e, i, o, and u. Let's see how many words we can find in five minutes that end in a vowel. I think you will find that words ending in i and u are the most difficult to find, so we will give three points for words ending in i and u and only one point for words ending in a, e, and o. For example, extra ends with an a and mine ends in e. We will allow proper names of people and places, but if you use a place be prepared to tell its location. If you are using a word that is new to you and may be new to the other players, be ready to define it so we can all learn together.

Take a sheet of paper and write the five vowels across the top of the sheet. Then as you find words, write them under the proper letter. Ready?

Teacher Reference List

a	e	i	o	u
Americana	accuse	alibi	bolo	Bantu
canna	ace	banzai	dado	ecru

Teacher Reference List (*cont.*)

a	e	i	o	u
cicada	ache	Delhi	halo	emu
extra	beige	ennui	hobo	gnu
fantasia	clique	etui	judo	Hindu
farina	due	gladioli	kayo	impromptu
flea	entire	Haiti	kimono	jujitsu
gala	flame	Heidi	lo	juju
Gaza	game	Hindustani	lotto	kudu
militia	home	karati	lumbago	lieu
Niagara	karate	kewi	mikado	Manchu
plea	mine	khaki	onto	milieu
pneumonia	there	lei	pogo	thou
quota	were	Magi	polo	thru
toga		martini	solo	virtu
ultra		Miami	tobacco	zebu
Victoria		Naomi	to	
viola		ski	too	
zebra		Tivoli	two	
		wapiti	veto	
			video	
			virtuoso	
			yahoo	

Note: The e list is a short one, since words in this category are the easiest to find. Understandably, words in the other four lists are not all familiar words, but with a dictionary as an aid this is not a problem. As in any dictionary word hunt, vocabularies should be considerably enlarged at the end of the game.

POKER FACE DEFINITIONS

Type of Game: Dictionary word
Play Method: Oral group

Grades: 4 and up

This is a better game for small groups than a whole class, but is not impossible as a class game.

Reading Directions

I will begin the game by selecting a word from the dictionary that you may or may not have heard of before. I will write it on the board for you to see. Then I will call on each player to give a definition of the word. If you have no idea of what it means, make up a definition. It may be an absolutely ridiculous one, but if you say it seriously, no one else will know whether you are bluffing or giving the actual meaning of the word. This is part of the fun of the game.

After every player has given his answer, I will read the correct definition and write it on the board. The player who gave the right definition gets the dictionary and picks out a new word for the rest to define. For example, I might pick the word *docent* for you to define. One of you might say it is "a small doe." Another might define it as "Norwegian money," while another could define it as "someone who is not decent." The actual definition of the word is "a teacher or lecturer not on the regular faculty."

I know you will find this a fun game. Try it at home with your friends or family. Remember, the word does not have to be a long word to make the game fun, but it must be an unusual word. Ready?

DIFFERENT ALIKES

Type of Game: Word classification   *Grades:*   3 and up
Play Method: Oral individual or written team

As an oral individual game: Name a key word and have the players volunteer to name the different kinds of things that word means. For example, the word might be "shoe." The players might name "people shoes," "horse shoes," "brake shoes," "toe-dancing shoes," etc.

As a written team game: Divide the group into small teams of five or six. Let each select a secretary-captain who records answers and adds his own contributions as well. At the end of a short time limit, let each captain read the list compiled by his team. Score a point for each correct classification.

Reading Directions

This is a word game in which we try to find as many possible different types of things that a word can mean. For example, I might give you the word *match*. Think how many kinds of matches we know about. There are wooden matches, paper matches, boxing matches, cricket matches, tennis matches, etc.

Some words, like the word *eyes*, apply to people, animals, birds, and things. So instead of naming every kind of people (men, women, children) or birds or animals, we will use only the one classification for each type and let one word cover one whole group. We will try to see how many different types we can think of for that word. Ready?

Teacher Reference List

Key Word	Classifications
1. pen	pig pen, ballpoint, quill, ink, felt, bullpen, playpen
2. foot or feet	people foot, animal foot, bird foot, foot of the table, foot of the river, linear foot, tenderfoot, foot in mouth, foot per second, foot of the mountains, foothills, claw foot, presser foot of a sewing machine
3. teeth or tooth	people, animal, shark, saw, false teeth, teeth of the wind, gear teeth, fork or rake teeth, sweet tooth, to put teeth in a law, tooth and nail, comb tooth, tooth of a leaf, armed to the teeth, skin of the teeth

4. tree — family tree, (growing) tree, clothes tree, shoe tree, whippletree, Christmas tree, gallows tree

5. glass or glasses — eyeglasses, spyglass, opera or field glasses, drinking glass, looking glass, window glass, barometer

6. star — star in sky, movie or TV star, stars in flag, general's star, stars in eyes, lucky stars, see stars after a blow, shooting star, pole star, star on face of horse

7. ring — bell ring, telephone ring, circus ring, finger ring, nose ring, bull ring, boxing ring, ring left by wet glass, annual tree ring, political ring, bathtub ring

8. pin — straight pin, safety pin, jewelry pin, cotter pin, bowling pin, clothespin, fraternity pin, hairpin or bobby pin, rolling pin

9. nail — toe- and fingernail, building nail, coffin (cigarette), hangnail

10. story — mystery story, picture story, fib type, joke type, news story, building floor

11. bird — feathered bird, badminton bird, bird in hand, birds of a feather, to give someone the bird

12. horse — animal horse, gymnastic horse, sawhorse, chess piece, clotheshorse

13. hook — fish hook, hook in boxing, clothes hook, bowling hook or golf hook

14. bed — sleeping bed, railroad bed, bed of flowers, bed rock (geological), put to bed (newspaper), wrong side of bed (irritable)

15. wheel — wheels on vehicles, steering wheel, potter's wheel, wheel maneuver (as in marching), wheels in air (bird movement), ship's wheel, spinning wheel

16. plate — home plate (baseball), false teeth plate, dinner plate, photographic plate, name for the anode (or positive element of an electron tube), horizontal wooden girder supporting the roof (in architecture)

17. shell — sea shell, egg or seed shell (outer coating), animal shell, empty shell, cartridge shell, shell one retreats into, hard shell people hide behind, pie shell

18. key   lock key, skate key, clock key, musical key, key to solution, keystone (architecture)

19. check   bank check, move in chess, identification item such as hat or baggage check, checks in paint, a cloth pattern, a mark denoting approval, a control area (check point), hold in check (restraint)

20. eye   people, animal, bird, fish, eye of the storm, eye on peacock's tail, eye in potatoes, needle eye, eyes of the law, bull's-eye in target, loop in a rope, fish-eye lens

Note: Suggest that players bring in other words that are fun to play with. Game could also be played using dictionaries.

Homographs and Homonyms

LOOK-ALIKE, SOUND-DIFFERENT WORDS

(HOMOGRAPHS)

Type of Game: Word   Grades: 4 and up
Play Method: Individual or team, oral or written

As an individual or team oral game: As a class game, write a word on the blackboard and ask for volunteers. Or divide the group into teams and call on volunteers from each team in rotation. A running score can be kept for teams.

As a written team game: Divide the group into teams, each with a captain. Each player has paper and pencil. Allow a limited time for writing answers, and after that time is up, have each captain collect the paper for his team. Then call on each captain, in turn, to read an answer. To keep interest high, keep a running score for each team.

Reading Directions

Some words are always pronounced the same. We have only to see the word and we know how to pronounce it. But certain other words are tricky. We must see these words in a sentence to know how they are to be pronounced. These words, called *homographs*, have different meanings and different pronunciations. Unless we see how the word is used in a sentence, we cannot be sure of the correct pronunciation. For example, take the letters *l-e-a-d*. What do they spell? Well, they actually spell two different words, which are pronounced differently. One is a verb, "It is my turn to *lead*." But *l-e-a-d* is pronounced differently if you are talking about making gold from *lead*.

Our game is to see how many words we can think of that are spelled the same but have different meanings and pronunciations. I have given you the two pronunciations and meanings of the words spelled *l-e-a-d*. In this example, one word is a verb, the other is a noun. Sometimes one word is an adjective and the second a verb. An example of this type of combination is *c-o-n-t-e-n-t; con-tent'*, the adjective; and *con'-tent*, the noun; and to make things even more confusing, *con-tent'*, the verb. To use all three in a sentence would sound like this: I am *content'* with the *con'tent* so I will *content'* myself with the results. Tricky? Yes, indeed.

Now, in five minutes, see how many such words you can list. Ready?

Teacher Reference List

Note: Accent marks are shown in syllabized words to help in correct pronunciation.

1. bass (bas) (*n*)	a type of fish; also the wood of the inner bark used for model building
bass (bās) (*n*)	the lowest male singing voice; the lowest-toned stringed instrument (*bass* viol)

2. bow (bou) (*vb*)   a greeting, nod of the head, sign of recognition, bend at the waist

   bow (bo) (*n*)   a knotted ribbon or material; a weapon used with an arrow; a playing stick for a stringed instrument such as a violin or cello

   bow (bou) (*n*)   the front part of a ship or airplane

3. con-serve' (*vb*)   to preserve; to keep in control so as not to waste, as to conserve a supply of food

   con'-serve (*n*)   a kind of jam or marmalade made with two or more fruits mixed together

4. con'-sole (*n*)   a type of table; the part of an organ that holds the keys; a floor cabinet for radio or phonograph

   con-sole' (*vb*)   to cheer or comfort pain, loss, or disappointment

5. con-sort' (*vb*)   to associate with; to join in agreement

   con'-sort (*n*)   marriage partner of the ruling king or queen, a partner or companion

6. con-tent' (*adj*)   the feeling of being satisfied with and not desiring better, to be replete

   con-tent' (*vb*)   to make oneself be satisfied, as "he *contented* himself"

   con'-tent (*n*)   that which is contained within a box, bottle, or any container; the main idea of a paper or poem; the amount of a particular ingredient or ingredients in a substance, as the water *content*

7. con-test' (*vb*)   to dispute, to bring legal action against

   con'-test (*n*)   a competition of strength, wits, or skill; a game or trial in which there is a competition to determine a winner

8. con'-voy (*n*)   a protective escort, a group traveling together for protection

   con-voy' (*vb*)   to act as a protective escort

9. de-sert' (*vb*)   to abandon
     de-sert' (*n*)   deserved punishment or reward
     des'-ert (*n*)   a sandy place
10. dove (duv) (*n*)   a type of pigeon
     dove (dov) (*vb*)   past tense of *dive*
11. house (hous) (*n*)   a dwelling for humans; a family group of royalty as "the *House* of Tudor"; the spectators in a theater; a shelter for animals, dog house; a part of Congress
     house (houz) (*vb*)   to give shelter, give housing to; to be housed in
12. in'-val-id (*n*)   a weak, sickly person
     in'-val-id (*adj*)   of or for invalids, as an *invalid* home
     in-val'id (*adj*)   null and void, having no force, not valid
13. live (liv) (*vb*)   to be alive; to maintain existence, as to *live* on one's pension
     live (liv) (*adj*)   glowing spark, as a *live* coal; available but unused, as *live* steam
14. min'-ute (*n*)   the sixtieth part of an hour; minutes, the record of a meeting
     mi-nute' (*adj*)   tiny, petty, trifling thing of little importance; marked by close attention to detail
15. mow (mo) (*vb*)   to harvest a crop by cutting with a hand tool or harvester; to defeat or destroy, as "*mow* down the opposition"
     mow (mou) (*n*)   a hayloft, part of the barn where hay is stored
16. ob'-ject (*n*)   a thing, a part of a sentence
     ob-ject' (*vb*)   to oppose, protest
17. pre-sent' (*vb*)   to offer a gift or honor, to introduce
     pres'-ent (*adj*)   in attendance
     pres'-ent (*n*)   a gift
18. pro'-gress (*n*)   a moving forward, an improvement
     pro-gress' (*vb*)   to move forward, to improve
19. pro'-ject (*n*)   an undertaking, goal, assignment

pro-ject' (vb)	to stick out; to propel forward; to make a picture appear on a screen by means of a projector; to make one's personality felt, as an actor *projects*
20. read (reed) (vb)	present tense, *to read*
read (red) (vb)	past tense of the same verb
21. rec'-ord (n)	an accounting of proceedings; a phonograph disc
re-cord' (vb)	to make notes of proceedings or transactions; to reproduce on a disc or wire or tape
rec'-ord (adj)	indicates something surpassed, as a *record* run or vote
22. re-fuse' (v)	to decline, reject
ref'-use (n)	rubbish, litter
23. row (ro) (vb)	to propel a boat with an oar; to engage in a boat race, as *row* a race
row (rou) (n)	a quarrel, noisy argument, disturbance
row (ro) (n)	a line-up of people, animals, or things, standing side by side
24. sow (so) (vb)	to scatter seed for planting purposes; to disseminate information
sow (sou) (n)	an adult female pig; in making pig iron, the channel in which the molten metal runs to the molds in which pig iron bars are made
25. tear (têr) (n)	a secretion of the eye gland; anything of a droplet shape
tear (târ) (vb)	to rip paper or cloth; to cut a jagged edge; to pull down or demolish, as "*tear* down a house"
tear (târ) (adj)	a printed sheet, part of an unbound manuscript
26. use (ūs) (n)	ability to put into service, having value, or being of use

use (uz) (vb)	to put into practice, to employ, to consume
27. wind (n)	current of air; breath, as in "to get second wind"; certain instruments in the orchestra; scent, as "a hunting dog keeps the wind"
wind (wīnd) (vb)	to wrap or roll something around itself or on a spool or drum; to tighten, as to wind a clock; to encircle, as to wind a bandage around an ankle; to weave in and out, as in dancing or as a stream winds; to twist or wind someone around one's finger
Other common words:	re′-bound (n), rē-bound′ (vb); re-call′ (vb), re′-call (n); re′-ject (n), re-ject′ (vb)

LOOK-ALIKE, SOUND-ALIKE WORDS (HOMONYMS)

Type of Game: Word   *Grades:* 4 and up
Play Method: Oral individual or team

As an individual game: Challenge the entire group, asking for volunteers for words. Write the answers on the blackboard to avoid duplication.

As a team game: Divide the group into teams and call on every member of each team in turn. Score one point for each correct answer.

Reading Directions

One kind of homonym is a word that sounds like another but is spelled differently. For example, p-e-a-r and p-a-r-e are spelled differently but are pronounced the same. Another kind is a word that is spelled like another but is pronounced differently, for example, *bow*. As the front of a ship it is pronounced like *cow*. As the *bow* tied in your shoelace, it is pronounced to rhyme with *show*. There is still another kind of homonym, the kind we are playing with today. This is the kind of word that is spelled and pronounced like another but has an entirely different meaning. In fact, in all three types of homonyms we have mentioned, the meanings of the words differ.

We are calling the type of homonyms we are playing with, sound-alike look-alike words. Take for example the word *b-e-a-r*. The noun *bear* is an animal. The verb *bear* means to carry. Even the verb *bear* has many meanings. We *bear* our burdens, we *bear* a grudge, a tree may *bear* fruit. When we push down hard on something, we *bear* down.

Not all look-alike sound-alike words are verb and noun combinations. They are sometimes verb and adjective combinations. An example of the verb-adjective combination is the word *f-a-s-t*. The adjective form means "quick, rapid." The verb *fast*, on the other hand, means to go without food or to abstain. To mix us up even further, if we use the verb meaning "to abstain" and put it with the word *day*, we have a *fast day*. In that expression we are using the verb meaning as an adjective. Just think how many meanings a simple little four-letter word can have!

To start the game, I will give you a word. Raise your hand if you can give the meaning or definition and the class of word you are defining. In other words, after the definition you must tell us if you are defining the verb, adjective, or noun form of the word. Later in the game, if you can think of this type of homonym, you may challenge us. Ready? The word is *b-a-l-l*.

Teacher Reference List

Word	Definitions
ball (n)	a round object; a rounded part, as *ball* of the foot, *ball* and socket joint; the eye*ball*; a piece of game

equipment, as base*ball,* soccer *ball,* etc.; a formal dance; a baseball thrown outside the strike zone

(vb)   to make something into a ball

bank *(n)*   a mound or a heap of earth, clouds, etc.; a row, as in a bench of rowers in a galley; a place for money transactions; a row of keys on an organ console; an array of lights on a playing field; place for keeping blood or corneal material, as an eye *bank*

(vb)   to deposit money; to heap ashes on a fire; to maneuver an airplane

bare *(adj)*   unclothed, uncovered, empty

(vb)   to strip, expose

can *(n)*   a container

(vb)   to preserve; also means to be able

care *(n)*   a concern, a worry, a weight on the mind, a trial, an interest

(vb)   to like or love; to be anxious or worried about; to assume responsibility for

cow *(n)*   female of cattle, elephants, buffalo, and whale

(vb)   to intimidate, to frighten into submission

die *(n)*   one of a pair of dice; a form for molding, or a stamp

(vb)   to stop living; to become fainter or weaker

dresser *(n)*   a valet, one who dresses another; description of a particular way someone dresses, as a fancy *dresser;* someone who arranges merchandise in a store window, a window *dresser;* a piece of furniture, a bureau; a table on which food is prepared for serving; a cupboard for dishes and utensils

drone *(n)*   a male honeybee; a loafer or idler; a radio-controlled, pilotless airplane; a bagpipe sound

(vb)   to make a humming, monotonous sound; to talk in a monotone

duck *(n)*   a water bird; a heavy cotton cloth similar to canvas

(vb)   to plunge into water, dipping under; to bend the head to avoid hitting an obstruction

fine *(n)*   money paid for an infraction of rules

fine (*adj*)	finished, good, perfect; keen, as a knife with a *fine* edge; opposite of *coarse*
grade (*n*)	mark or rating on an exam; a sloping area; a division in a school
(*vb*)	to change the level, as to *grade* a road; to mark or evaluate, as to *grade* papers
hail (*n*)	frozen raindrops; a form of greeting
(*vb*)	to shout a greeting; a method of signaling, as to *hail* a taxi; to come from a particular place
long (*adj*)	lengthy, as in expression "so *long*"
(*vb*)	to yearn
low (*adj*)	of little height, not high or tall
(*vb*)	to moo like a cow
rose (*n*)	a flower; a color
(*vb*)	the past tense of *rise*
tax (*n*)	a revenue levied on property, income, or goods
(*vb*)	to request payment; to overexert or strain
tie (*n*)	a link or connection, as family *ties*; a neck *tie*; part of a railroad bed; a stalemate or even score
(*vb*)	to fasten or bind together; to make a knot
time (*n*)	tempo; a period of interval of the day, year, or era; a prison sentence; a rate of speed; a repeated instance, as *time* after *time*; a system of measurement; to be cautious as in to take *time*
(*adj*)	describing a method of paying on installments, as a *time* payment; set to explode after a certain interval, as a *time* bomb; of or relating to time, a *time* interval
(*vb*)	to measure an interval, as to *time* a runner
tire (*n*)	iron or rubber around a wheel
(*vb*)	to weaken; to lose interest, to lose patience
train (*n*)	part of a dress; connected line of cars
(*vb*)	to instruct; to undergo physical discipline for sports

Other common words in this category:

bark	bob	buck	card	date	diet
bay	box	cape	dam	deed	foil

fold	mine	plum	rent	seal
fork	mint	pound	ring	tick
mean	pants	race	ruler	tire

Variation: Play as a dictionary word hunt. Let each player find a word and be prepared to give its many meanings when called upon. To avoid duplication, give every two or three children a different letter of the alphabet to work with. Thus you will have many different words from all sections of the dictionary. Call on as many players as possible in the game period. Those left over can be called on in days to come.

SOUND-ALIKE, SPELLED-DIFFERENTLY WORDS (HOMONYMS)

Type of Game: Word   Grades: 3 and up
Play Method: Individual or team, oral or written

As an oral or written individual game: Challenge the class, calling on volunteers, who must spell the word combinations they volunteer. As a written game, allow three to five minutes for players to work on a list. Then call on individuals in turn to give one example on their lists. Write the words on the blackboard to avoid duplications.

As a written team game: Divide the group into teams, each with a secretary-captain who records the words volunteered by his teammates and adds his own contributions as well. At the end of the time limit, call on each captain in turn to give a word combination from his list. Write these on the blackboard to avoid duplication. Keep a team score, giving one point for each correctly spelled word.

Reading Directions

There are several types of homonyms. Some are words that sound like others but are spelled differently and, of course, have different meanings. This is the type we are playing with in this game. For example, here are two words that are pronounced the same but are not spelled the same, s-u-m and s-o-m-e. Another example combination is b-e-a-r and b-a-r-e.

Let's see how many different homonym combinations we can name in five minutes. Remember that in some cases there may be three words instead of two. Anyone may volunteer a combination and I will write it on the board so that we won't be repeating. Be prepared to define or give the meaning of the words you give me. Ready?

Teacher Reference List

air, heir, ere	feat, feet	presence, presents
alter, altar	flee, flea	prey, pray
assent, ascent	fore, for, four	principal, principle
awl, all	great, grate	raze, raise
bear, bare	hear, here	real, reel
beat, beet	heart, hart	reign, rain, rein
bow, bough	herd, heard	rite, right
buy, by, bye	horse, hoarse	rumor, roomer
capitol, capital	lead, led	sail, sale
cents, sense, scents	mail, male	scene, seen
chilly, chili	mane, main	sea, see
coarse, course	mantle, mantel	seam, seem
desert (vb), dessert	meat, meet	seize, sees
do, dew, due	morning, mourning	slay, sleigh
dual, duel	or, oar, ore	some, sum
dye, die	pale, pail	to, too, two
eight, ate	peel, peal	toe, tow
ewe, you	plain, plane	ware, wear
eye, aye	pore, pour	won, one
fair, fare		

Note: Encourage the player to bring combinations to class when they come across a new one. Suggest this as a game to play while car or bus riding, or to make a waiting period seem shorter.

Variation #1: See also the game "Teakettle" (page 123) below, another homonym word game.

Variation #2: Play as a group game; write one homonym on the board and then ask for answers from individuals in the group for the second or third word in that set.

Variation #3: Play as a blackboard game. Organize the group into teams. Write one word on the board and ask for a volunteer from the first team for the second homonym in that series. If there is a third, a player on the second team is asked. If no one on a team can answer, the play goes to the next team. Score a point for a correct answer. When all the words in that combination have been given, begin a new combination.

With older players, a player in turn names one of a combination of homonyms. The next player names another in that group. When a group is completed, the next player must begin a new combination. In other words, supply no words for this game; the players must do all the work. Do, however, record the words on the blackboard to avoid duplication and argument.

TEAKETTLE

Type of Game: Trick word (homonym)
Grades: 3 and up
Play Method: Oral individual or written team

As an oral individual game: As an individual game, one player challenges the entire group. The player who guesses the right answer challenges the group with his own sentence.

As a written team game: Divide the group into teams, each with a captain-secretary who records the contributions of his teammates and adds his own. Then call on the first team to give a sentence. The first team to identify the synonyms then gives one of its own as a challenge. Since each team has compiled a list, it is likely that one or more have come up with the same combinations and will be able to identify the challenger's on their own list.

Reading Directions

This is a trick word game using homonyms—in this case, words that sound alike but are spelled differently. An example is the combination, g-r-e-a-t and g-r-a-t-e. Using this combination in a trick sentence, I would substitute the word *teakettle* for each of the homonyms. For example, I might say, "The *teakettle* gave off a *teakettle* heat." (The *grate* gave off a *great* heat.) Or I might say, "*Teakettle* scott, the *teakettle* is cold!" (*Great* scott, the *grate* is cold!)

Anyone who guesses the words *teakettle* is substituting for, challenges the rest of the group with a sentence of his own. Let's take a minute for each of you to make a little list of your own homonyms, so that if you guess correctly you will be ready to give another quickly. Keep your lists and keep adding to them as you think of other combinations, so we can play this game again. Try playing it at home with your family or friends. It is a good party game or one to play on a bus or in a car.

I will start you out with a sentence now. The first to guess will give one of his own. Ready? My sentence is:

"Have you ever seen a teakettle teakettle?" (A bare bear.)

Teacher Reference List

See list of homonyms given in the game "Sound-Alike, Spelled-Differently Words," page 122.

Letters and Syllables

CONSONANT FUN

Type of Game: Word   Grades: 3 and up
Play Method: Individual or team, oral or written (also dictionary hunt)

As an individual game: As an oral game, ask for volunteers from the class and write the suggested word on the board as the player spells it. Corrections in spelling are made, if necessary, by volunteers from the class.

As a written game, each player writes a list. At the end of the time limit, players are called on in turn to give a word, which is then written on the blackboard to avoid duplication.

As a team game: As an oral game, call a member from each team in turn and write the word on the blackboard, scoring points for each correct word and giving an extra point for one correctly spelled. Team scores are kept to add to the fun.

As a written game, divide the group into teams, each with a captain-secretary, who records the suggestions from his teammates, making his own contributions as well. At the end of the time period, call on each captain in turn, asking for a single word at a time.

Score a point for each correct word and an extra point if it is correctly spelled.

Reading Directions

Consonants are those letters in the alphabet that are not vowels. In this particular game we are looking for words that have a doubled consonant in them. These may come within the word, and at the end, and very rarely at the beginning. For example, we want such words as *tattle* which has a doubled *t* within the word, or success which has both a doubled s at the end and a doubled c within it. There are only a few that have a doubled consonant at the beginning, and these all begin with l. Llama is an example. You will find a few others in the dictionary. Since we have limited time to play, let's begin with the first five consonants in the alphabet and try to find words that come under each. We will be looking for words with a b-b, c-c, d-d, f-f, or g-g in them somewhere.

Note: At another time use the next set of letters. There are no hh, jj, kk, and xx words, but it is fun to throw one such request in for the fun of it and let the players find out for themselves.

Teacher Reference List

BB	CC	DD	FF
abba	accelerate	daddy	afflict
abbess	accent	dodder	afford
abbey	accept	eddy	baffle
abbreviate	access	faddist	baffling
babble	accessory	fiddle	coefficient
cabbage	accident	fodder	coffee
cabby	accord	giddy	differ
dabble	baccalaureate	gladden	efface
ebb	eccentric	huddle	effect
flabby	flaccid	ladder	efficient
gabber	hiccup	laddie	fluff
grubby	moccasin	meddle	gaff
hobble		middle	giraffe
hobby	DD	paddle	muffin
hubbub	add	peddle	muffle
jabber	adder		
jobber	addict	FF	GG
knobby	addition	affair	aggress
pebble	coddle	affect	aggression
		affix	aggrieve

baggage
baggy
cogged
dagger
digger
druggist
egg
flagging
flogger
foggy
gagged
giggle
goggle
haggle
jigger
jiggle
joggle
juggle
lagging
logger
luggage
muggy
piggy

LL

all
allege
allegiance
alleviate
alley
artillery
ball
ballad
ballast
ballistic
balloon
ballot

call
calla
callous
callus
college
collegiate
collier
dell
dill
drill
dwell
ellipse
faille
fall
fallow
fell
fellow
fill
follow
full
gall
gallery
gallon
gallop
gorilla
gully
hello
hill
holly
hull
ill
illegal
jelly
kill
killer
llama
lull

mall
mallet
mellow
mill
million
pellet
pill
poll

MM

ammonia
chummy
commander
commend
common
communicate
dimmer
drummer
dummy
gamma
gammon
gimmick
grammar
grimmer
hammer
hammock
hemming
humming
immediate
lummox
mamma
mummy
rummy

NN

inning
inn

annex
annoy
announce
annual
annul
banner
banns
canna
cannibal
canned
cannon
chinning
Cincinnati
cinnamon
connect
connive
dinner
ennoble
ennui
Finn
finnan
finnicky
flannel
funnel
funny
granny
gunner
gunny
henna
hinny
manna
manner
minnow
pennant

PP

appall

Teacher Reference List (*cont.*)

PP

apparatus
apparel
apparent
appeal
apple
choppy
copper
dapper
dapple
dipper
dripping
flapper
flippant
flipper
flopping
foppish
grapple
grippe
gripping
guppy
happen
happy
hipped
hippo
lapped
opportunity
pepper

RR

arrange
array
arrest
arrival

barrack
barracuda
barrage
barred
barrel
barren
barrier
carriage
carrier
carrion
carrot
carry
cirrus
correct
correspond
derrick
err
errant
error
farrow
ferry
furrier
furry
garret
garrote
gerrymander
herring
horrid
horror
hurry
irradiate
irritate
lorry
marriage

marry
merry
mirror
morrow
narrate
narrative
parrot

SS

access
address
assail
assent
assert
bass
bassoon
casserole
cassock
class
Cossack
cross
dessert
dissemble
dissent
dissipate
dress
essay
essence
essential
fission
fissure
floss
fossil
gassy

glass
glossy
gossip
grass
hassle
hiss
issue
kiss
lass
less
loss
mass
massive
message
messy
mission
moss
muss
passive
stress

TT

attach
attack
attain
attempt
attend
batten
batter
battery
cattle
catty
clatter
cotter

cotton	hitter	divvy	fezzes
cutter	jitter	chivvy	fizzle
ditto	kitty	civvies	fizzy
fatten	knotter		frazzle
fettle	latter	**WW**	fuzz
fitter	lattice	bowwow	fuzzy
fitting	letter	glowworm	grizzle
flatter	litter	powwow	grizzly
flutter	little		guzzle
fritter	matter	**ZZ**	huzzah
gavotte	motto	blizzard	izzard
getting	otter	buzz	jazz
ghetto	petty	buzzard	mezzanine
glitter	scuttle	buzzer	mezzotint
glutton		dizziness	nozzle
gritty	**VV**	dizzy	razzle-dazzle
gutter	divvies	drizzle	

Variation: When played as a dictionary word hunt team game, suggest that each team member hunt under a different letter to avoid wasting time with duplication. There are no *hh, jj, kk,* or *xx* words but throw one of these classifications in to let the players find out that for themselves. As in the original directions, limit the doubled consonants in the game to five or six at a time. You can always try a new set for another time.

When strange words are used, tell players that they will be expected to give definitions. When geographical names are used, players will be expected to locate the places in brief terms.

DOUBLE- AND TRIPLE-LETTER WORD FUN

Type of Game: Word   *Grades:*   4 and up
Play Method: Oral individual or written team

As an oral individual game: After reading the game explanation, ask players to volunteer words, and then write them on the board.

As a written team game: Divide the group into teams by row or groups. Let each team select a captain-secretary, who will write the suggestions volunteered by his teammates and add his own suggestions as well. At the end of the time limit, call on the captains in turn to give one word at a time. Write the words on the board to avoid duplications. The team with the most words wins.

Reading Directions

There are certain letters in the alphabet that sound like words, like C and U, while other letters are actually words, like I and a. If we combine letters like this we make other words. For example, the letters I and C when put together sound like icy. K and T make a girl's name, Katie. In some cases we can put three letters together and make a word; for example, M-L-E make a girl's name, Emily. N-M-E sounds like enemy. Sometimes if we put two of the same letters together we get a word. Two Us (U-U) sounds like u-s-e, and two Ys (Y-Y) sounds like w-i-s-e.

Let's see how many double- or triple-letter words we can name. Incidentally, this is a good game to try on your friends or at home. Try it while riding the school bus. It will make the trip home shorter.

A hint on how to find the letter words. Take a letter of the alphabet and put it in front of each letter in turn saying it quietly to yourself, as, for example, A-A, A-B. There, you see you have a boy's name, Abie. When you have gone all through the alphabet with one letter, try another. Ready?

Teacher Reference List

Two-letter words	Meanings
AB	Abie
BB (Bs)	bees
BZ	busy
CC (Cs)	sees, seas, seize
CN	seein', scene
CR	seer, sear
CT	city
DK	decay
DT	ditty
DZ	dizzy
EE (Es)	ease
EZ	easy
FE	Effie
II (Is)	eyes
IL	aisle, isle
IV	ivy
JL	jail
KC	Casey
KG	cagey
KL	kale
LC	Elsie
LE	Ellie
LI	ally
LL (Ls)	else
LN	Ellen
LX	Alex
MA	Emmae
MC	emcee
ME	Emmie
MT	empty

Teacher Reference List (*cont.*)

Two-letter words	Meanings
NE	any
NV	envy
OK	okay
ON	Owen
OO (Os)	owes
PT	Petie
PP (Ps)	peas
PT	pity
PU	phew
QQ (Qs)	queues
RI	awry
RT	Artie
SA	essay
SX	Essex
TL	teal
TP	teepee
TT (Ts)	tees, tease
UL	yule
UU (Us)	ewes, use, yews
WW (Ws)	double use
XL	excel
YY (Ys)	wise
ZL	zeal

Three-letter Words	Meanings
CCS (CsS)	seizes
CCN (CsN)	season
CCR (CsR)	Caesar
EEL (EsL)	easel
EES (EsS)	eases
FEG	effigy

INN (INs)	ions
LEG	elegy
LIS	Elias
NDN	Indian
NME	enemy
NRG	energy
NTT	entity
NUE	ennui
NVR	envier
NVS	envious
NVV (NVs)	envies
SNN (SNs)	essence
TTR (TsR)	teaser
VVA (VsA)	visa
XTC	ecstasy

Four-letter Words	Meanings
CCNL (CsNL)	seasonal
UBQT	ubiquity
UUUR (UsUR)	usurer

Variation: Now try letters and numbers together to make words. The numbers that make words are given below.

Teacher Reference List

Number Words	Meanings
1	won
2	too, to
4	for, fore
8	ate
¼	fourth

Letter and Number Words	Meanings
4A	foray
NE1	anyone

Teacher Reference List (*cont.*)

Letter and Number Words	Meanings
7T	seventy
8T	eighty
9T	ninety
4T	forty
6T	sixty
2N, 2NN (2Ns)	tune, tunes
2L, 2LL (2Ls)	tool, tools
4C	foresee
4CC	foresees
4N	foreign
4¼	forequarter
4TT (4Ts)	forties
8TT (8Ts)	eighties
9TT (9Ts)	nineties
6TT (6Ts)	sixties
7TT (7Ts)	seventies
B4	before
B½	behalf
U4EA	euphoria
MN8	emanate
N44 (N4s)	enforce
LF8R	elevator
XP8	expiate
XP8R	expiator

Variation: When the players become proficient in the use of letter and number words, have them make sentences. Encourage the players to make up some at home to bring to class and challenge the rest of the group. Such a sentence written on the board will be good seat-problem fun for odd moments.

WORD GAMES 135

Sentence Examples

I C 2 NDNN (NDNs).   I see two Indians.

RT TTS (TsS) ON.   Artie teases Owen.

B4 U TT (Ts) LC BYY (BYs).   Before you tease Elsie be wise.

I C 2 NDN TPP (TPs).   I see two Indian teepees.

R U DZ, 2?   Are you dizzy, too?

ON NVV (NVs) LEE (LEs) NRG.   Owen envies Ellie's energy.

BB (Bs) R YY (Ys).   I C U R YY (Ys), 2.   Bees are wise. I see
you are wise, too.

I TT (Ts) U.   I tease you.

U 8 BB (Bs)?   R U DZ?   You ate bees? Are you dizzy?

EASY(?) WORD GAME

Type of Game: Word   *Grades:* 3 and up
Play Method: Individual or team, oral or written

As an individual oral or written game: Ask the players to volunteer answers, giving the required type of word, spelling it,
and defining it when asked to. The teacher writes the word on
the board. As a written game, have the players, in a limited
time, write as many words as possible. Call on players, in rotation, and write words on the blackboard to avoid duplication.

As a team game: Divide the group into teams, with a captain-
secretary who writes the words suggested by his teammates and
makes his own contributions as well. Call on team captains
alternately to read a word from their lists. Put these on the
board. Score a point for each correctly spelled word.

Reading Directions

Writing three-letter words sounds like an easy thing to do.
See how many words you can write in five minutes. They must
be correctly spelled and you must be able to tell what they
mean. No proper names, please. Ready?

Teacher Reference List

ado	bad	cob	due	fie	row
adz	bah	cot	dun	fin	sod
alp	ban	coy	duo	foe	too
apt	bat	cue	dye	ire	tow
arc	bid	cur	eel	irk	two
ark	boa	dam	eke	job	vie
asp	bob	die	elf	ken	vug
ave	box	din	emu	low	wen
awe	bun	don	era	mow	
awl	cad	dub	err	oaf	
aye	cam	dud	eve	oat	

Variation #1: Play using four-letter words as the challenge.

Teacher Reference List

ache	alms	bale	bubo	deft	flow
acid	ante	bass	burr	dido	fret
aeon	arid	bear	clan	dote	kiwi
agog	atom	bleb	clef	dupe	kudu
aide	awry	bole	cote	emit	leek
ajar	axle	bout	cyst	épée	neon
ally	bade	brig	dais	ever	zebu

Variation #2: Ask for a three- and four-letter word for every letter of the alphabet.

Teacher Reference List

Three-letter Words			Four-letter Words		
A	awe	ark	A	ache	acid
B	ban	bid	B	burr	bole
C	cad	cot	C	clef	come
D	dun	dot	D	dote	dupe
E	eke	ewe	E	ever	emus
F	fie	fin	F	floe	fret

Three-letter Words				*Four-letter Words*			
G	gel	gee	gnu	G	gene	gram	
H	ham	hem		H	hake	hack	
I	irk	ire	imp	I	idyl	idea	ibid
J	jag	jam		J	jade	jape	
K	keg	key		K	keel	kelp	
L	lip	lag		L	lime	lieu	
M	mad	mud		M	Magi	maim	malt
N	nag	neb		N	nape	neon	
O	orb	oaf	ode	obi	O	oath	oboe	ogle
P	par	pad		P	pant	part	pawn
Q	qua	quo		Q	quiz	quip	
R	rap	raw	rip	R	rack	rank	reek
S	sac	spa	ski	S	saga	scan	seer
T	tab	taw		T	talc	tear	
U	urn	ugh		U	undo	ulna	ugly
V	vie	van	vex	V	vamp	veil	vane
W	wag	wan		W	wake	wale	walk
X				X	x-ray	Xmas	
Y	yak	yaw	yea	Y	yegg	yaws	yawl
Z	zed	zip		Z	zeal	zinc	zebu

Variation #3: Write several three- or four-letter words on the blackboard and have players either individually or by teams write the definitions.

Variation #4: On the blackboard, write three- or four-letter words that are unfamiliar, or familiar words that have many meanings. Let the players, individually or by teams (each player with his own dictionary), look up the meanings of unfamiliar words. Use reference lists of three- and four-letter words that include some unfamiliar words.

Variation #5: Ask for definitions of five-letter words. Make this a dictionary game, if necessary.

Teacher Reference List (Five-Letter Words)

abhor	agape	besom
abode	allot	cache
acrid	aloof	comer
adobe	aspen	dogie
afoul	avast	eyrie

Variation #6:   Ask for five- or six-letter words, each beginning with a different letter of the alphabet. Make this a dictionary hunt. Players must be prepared to define unusual or new words.

LETTER WORD FUN

Type of Game: Word   *Grades:*   3 and up
Play Method: Oral or written team game

As an oral game: Read the game directions, challenging the group to think of answers. Select volunteers at random and write the correct answers on the board for the others to see.

As a written game: Divide the class into teams by rows or groups. Have each team select a captain-secretary. At the signal to begin, players suggest answers to the captain, who writes them down and also makes contributions of his own. At the end of the time allotted, team captains read aloud their lists. The team with the longest correct list wins.

Reading Directions

Today our game deals with letters of the alphabet that sound like and sometimes are words. The letter *I* is a personal pronoun that all of you know. The letter *B* sounds like two different words, *be*, the verb, and *bee*, the insect.

Let's see how many letter words we can find. I will write them on the board as they are named. As you can see by the example, some letters sound like more than one word, so try to name all the words that particular letter sounds like.

Teacher Reference List

Letter	Word
A	(article)
B	be, bee
C	see, sea
D	Dee (a river in Scotland)
G	gee (word of command to horse or ox: turn to right or go ahead, gee-up)
I	(pronoun)
J	jay (bird)
K	Kay (a girl's nickname)
L	ell (a wing of a building; a former measure of length)
M	em (a unit of measure in printing—a square of any size of type)
N	en (a unit of measure in printing—an en is half an em)
O	O, oh (an expression of fear, wonder, pain, or surprise)
P	pea
R	are
T	tee, tea
U	you
X	?eggs? (a fun way of using)
Y	why

Variation #1:   Let the players use the letter words in a sentence.

Teacher Reference List

I C A B.   U C A C.   O, I C Y U R.
U C A B.   I C A J.
R U A B?   U C A J.
O, I C Y.   I C A B. O!
O, I C A C.

Variation #2: Add numbers that sound like words.

Teacher Reference List

1   won
2   too, to
4   for, fore
8   ate

Variation #3: Now try putting letter words and number words together to make sentences.

I 8 A B.   I C K.
I 8 A B, 2.   I C A T, 2.
O, I C U 8 A B, 2.   I C A C.
A J 8 A B, 2.
K 8 A B, 2.   U C A C, 2?
I C 1 T.
I C A T, 2.

Variation #4: See "Double-Letter Word Fun" (page 129), a more complicated game for older players.

SILLY SYLLABLES

Type of Game: Word trick   *Grades:* 4 and up
Play Method: Oral group

This is a group game, with anyone volunteering the answer.

Reading Directions

We have talked in class of the importance of breaking a word into its proper syllables. This game of silly syllables shows you what happens if you aren't careful.

I am going to spell out a series of words. After each word I will ask for a volunteer to pronounce the word. I will break each word into syllables in a tricky way. Let's see if I can trick you. Ready? The first word is h-a-t-b-a-n-d. (*Note: In spelling out the trick word make a pause at the asterisk, though this is not the correct place for a pause.*)

Ready? The first word is *h-a-t*b-a-n-d*. Right, the word is *hatband*. Second word, *h-a-t*r-a-c-k*. *Hatrack* it is. Next word is *h-a-t*r-e-d*. Oops! See what happens when we syllabize incorrectly?

Teacher Reference List

Mc*Carthy, Mac*Duff, mac*aroni, mac*hine
col*lar, col*league, col*lie, col*onel
car*ry, car*rot, car*ving
cup*ful, cup*board, cup*id
ant*eater, ant*acid, ant*ler, ant*hem
tow*head, tow*hee, tow*line, tow*els, tow*ard
can*cel, can*non, can*cer, can*als
com*bat, com*bine, com*bings
anti*freeze, anti*knock, anti*ques
bal*last, bal*lot, bal*let, bal*miness
as*sume, as*ter, as*sure, as*ylum
ath*letic, ath*lete, Ath*ens, ath*ome
at*om, at*tain, at*tract, at*witter
auto*clave, auto*graph, auto*mat, auto*nomy
ava*lanche, ava*rice, ava*unt
aw*ful, aw*ning, aw*ry or aw*oken
Bac*chus, bac*teria, bac*king, bac*helor

cal*lus, Cal*vary, Cal*vin, cal*ves
Han*cock, han*dle, han*som, han*ger
has*sle, has*sock, has*ten, has*hsish
hum*ble, hum*bug, hum*ans, hum*ane, hum*or
Is*abel, Is*rael, is*land
it*chy, it*self, It*aly, it*ems
lu*nar, lu*cid, lu*cky
mat*ter, mat*ting, mat*ron
mole*hill, mole*skin, mole*ster
se*clude, se*cede, se*cond, se*cular
e*lope, e*lude, e*loquent
en*able, en*act, en*ough

SYLLABLE SOUNDS

Type of Game: Word   Grades: 3 and up
Play Method: Oral or written, individual or team

As a written team game: Organize the class into small groups, with a captain-secretary for each. The captain-secretary will record the words volunteered by his teammates, adding his own contributions as well.

As an oral game: Present the problem and call for volunteers from the class. Write correct answers on the blackboard for the others to see so that duplications can be avoided. The players will soon understand that even though syllables look the same, they are often pronounced in several different ways.

Reading Directions
Syllables are very tricky things. All syllables that are spelled the same may be pronounced four or five different ways, depending on the word in which they appear. For example, the o-w in cow is pronounced differently than the o-w in show. Let's

see how many words we can name which have the *ow* sound of *cow* and the *ow* of *show*. I will make two columns on the board, one with the *ow* sound of *cow*, the second with the *ow* of *show*. Let's see how many words we can put under each.

There is another interesting thing to remember. Some syllables may look alike, but are not pronounced the same. Some words, called homonyms, can be spelled alike but pronounced differently. So a word like *s-o-w* can be pronounced like *cow* and also like *show*, since the words have different meanings and derivatives, or beginnings. Words such as these can be listed under each column. Watch for words like these.

Teacher Reference List

ow as in cow		ow as in show	
allow	kowtow	below	owing
bow	now	blow	own
bower	owl	bow	ownership
clown	plow	flow	row
dowel	pow	flown	slow
dowry	row	glow	sow
down	sow	grow	stow
endow	towel	know	throw
flower	tower	low	
haymow	town	mow	
how	vow	owe	
	vowel		

Variation #1: With the *o-n* syllable, there are five different possible sounds.

1. The *o-n* as in *done* (un)
2. The *o-n* as in *gone* (awn)
3. the *o-n* as in *bone* (oh)
4. the *o-n* as in *concert* (on)
5. the *o-n* as in *condemn* (ən)

Teacher Reference List

done (un)

bonita
button
conceal
conceit
conceive
console
contrive
honey
money
one
oneness
son
sponge
ton
tongue
won
wonder

gone (awn)

dong
goner
gong
honk
long
longhorn
prong
song
songbird
songster
strong

thong
throng
tong
wrong
wrongful

bone (oh)

alone
atone
atonement
bonemeal
boner
bonus
bony
cone
coney
donate
donor
don't
lone
only
phone
pony
prone
pronoun
pronounce
shone
sonar
stone
throne
tone
zone

concert (on)

bronze
concave
concentrate
concentration
concourse
concrete
conduct
confide
congress
conk
conquer
constable
Donald
donkey
fond
fondant
font
gondola
Hong Kong
honky-tonk
honor
honorable
ionic
ironic
longitude
nonsense
onset
onside
onto
onyx
pontiff

pontoon
pronto
rondo
sonic
sponsor
tonic
yonder

condemn (ən)

concern
confess
confetti
confirm
conform
confuse
congeal
congenial
connect
consist
console
conspire
construct
ion
ionize
monopoly
monotonous
sonata

Variation #2:   The e-n sounds are also variable. These divide into five different sounds:

1. the e-n as in *endure* (in)
2. the e-n as in *end* (en)
3. the e-n as in *ensemble* (ën)
4. The e-n as in *genial* (ēn)
5. The e-n as in *even* (ən)

Teacher Reference List

endure (in)	*end* (en)	
enact	bench	envy
enfold	bend	event
engage	benefit	fence
engrain	Benjamin	fend
engrave	cent	fender
engulf	center	general
enjoy	central	gentle
enlarge	century	glen
enrage	clench	hence
enrich	denim	incense
enroll	dentist	kennel
enslave	enchant	mend
ensue	energetic	mental
entail	engine	open
enthuse	engineer	pen
enthusiasm	enmity	penalty
entire	enter	pencil
entitle	entertain	pending
entrench	entity	penitence
envelop	entry	plenty
	envelope	rent
	envelopment	send
	envoy	sense

end (en)	ensemble (ën)	genial (en)	even (ən)
sent	ennui	genius	even
stenotype	envelope	keno	evenness
tendency		penal	evensong
tent		penalize	Kentucky
then		senile	peninsula
trench		senior	
uneven		venal	
when		zenith	

Variation #3:   Play this as a dictionary word hunt. The players will not only learn new words, but will learn to recognize pronunciation symbols as well.

Variation #4:   Play with words that have the *aw* in *awl* sound. Oddly enough, there are no other pronunciations for this syllable. Let the players find this out for themselves.

VOWEL COMBINATION FUN

Type of Game: Word   *Grades:*   4 and up
Play Method: Oral or written, individual or team

As an individual game: Ask for volunteers for words and write them on the blackboard, asking the player to spell the word. As a written game, have the individual players compile lists in a limited time period. Call on players in turn to give a word and spell it. If the words are written on the board as they are given, duplicates are avoided.

As a team game: Divide the group into teams, each with a captain-secretary who records the words suggested by his teammates and adds his own contributions as well. Can be played as a dictionary treasure hunt.

Reading Directions

We all know the vowels, a, e, i, o, and u. Sometimes they appear alone in a word, as the e appears in let. Sometimes they appear in combinations as i-e, i-o, o-u, a-i, a-e and so on. We are looking for vowels appearing in combinations. (Here, give five selected combinations. The reference list gives words in all possible combinations.) Let's begin with the a combinations. For example, an a-e word would be algae, an a-i word would be rain. The most difficult of these combinations to find words for will be the a-o combination. We will give three points for words in that list and one point for words with the other combinations. You may use proper names, but you must be able to locate geographical names or give meanings of strange words, which may be new to many players. That way we all learn together. Ready?

Teacher Reference List

ae		ai		ao	au
ae	paean	fairy	quail	**Maori**	
aegis	tael	faith	quaint	Naomi	
aeon		gaily	raid		
aerator	**ai**	gain	rail	**au**	
aerobatics	airplane	gait	rain		bauble
aeronaut	airy	hail	sail		Baum
Aesop	aisle	jail	tail		caucus
aesthetic	bail	kaiser	taint		caught
algae	daily	lair	vail		cause
amoebae	dainty	maid	vain		causeway
Caesar	dairy	mail			caustic
gaegar (gull)	daisy	main	**ao**		daub
Gaelic	faint	nail	kaolin		daughter
maelstrom	fair	pail	Laos		daunt

au	*ea*		*ei*	*eu*
faucet	area	seat		Beulah
fault	each	teal		deuce
fraud	ear	team		Deutschland
fraught	earl	tear		eugenics
gaudy	earth	tease		eureka
gauge	easel	unearned		eurythmic
gauze	fear	unearth		Europe
haunch	feat	uneasy		feud
haunt	feather	veal		neuter
jaundice	gear	wear		neutral
jaunt	head	weather		neutron
laud	hear	wheat		pneumonia
laugh	heat	yea		pseudonym
laundry	idea	year		reunion
laurel	ideal	yearn		reunite
maul	leaf	yeast		Teuton
mauve	mean	zeal		therapeutic
naught	near	Zealand		
naughty	neat	zealot		*ia*
pauper	peace	zealous		bias
pause	peach			diabetic
raucous	pear		*ei*	diadem
sauce	peat		being	diagnose
saucer	plea		ceiling	diagram
sauerkraut	queasy		deify	dial
sauna	real		deign	dialect
taunt	realize		eight	dialogue
taut	rear		eighty	diameter
vaudeville	reason		either	diamond
vault	seal		feign	diaper
vaunt	seam		feint	fiancé
	sear		heifer	fiat
			height	

heir
heirloom
leisure
neighbor
neither
reign
rein
seismograph
veil

eo

Cleopatra
Creole
creosote
deodorant
deodorize
Eolithic
eon
geography
geometry
geophysical
George
jeopardy
leopard
leotard
meow
neon
peon
peony
people
reopen
reorder
reorganize
theory

gentian
giant
glacial
gladiator
Hiawatha
liable
liaison
Miami
Niagara
variable

ie

alien
anxiety
belief
believe
bier
client
die
diesel
diet
fiend
fried
friend
fiery
gie
lie
lien
mien
niece
pie
piece
pier
relief

siesta
sieve
society
tie
tier
varied
variety
view

io

ambitious
attention
axiom
explosion
fiord
flexion
idiom
idiot
ion
kiosk
lion
pioneer
pious
Rio
riot
Sioux
sociology
trio
union
various

iu

helium
tedium

triumph
triumphant
triumvirate
uranium

oa

boat
coat
foal
goal
goat
hoary
koala
loaf
loan
loathe
moan
moat
Noah
oasis
oat
oath
roar
roast
soap
toast

oe

amoeba
doe
foe
hoe
noel
poem

poet
roe
roebuck
soever
toe

oi

boil
broil
coin
embroil
foist
going
groin
hoist
join
joint
loin
loiter
noisy
oil
point
soil
turmoil

ou

doubt
famous
flounder
foul
found
four
ghoul
gouge

gourd
gout
ground
hound
house
journal
journey
louse
out
snout
sound
though
wound

ua

casual
dual
equal
equate
Guam
guarantee
guard
guardian
Juan
obituary
persuasion
quart
quarter
quartz
quasi
suave
truant
unequal
unusual

	guerrilla		quit
ua	guess	*ui*	quiver
usual	hue	fluid	ruin
	Pueblo	fruit	suit
ue	queen	guide	tuition
blue	quench	guild	
clue	query	guilt	*uo*
cruel	question	guise	liquor
due	queue	juice	quoit
duel	roquet	liquid	quorum
fluent	rue	liquidate	quota
fuel	sue	nuisance	quote
gruel	true	quiet	quotient

Sensory Games

SENSE SENTENCES

Type of Game: Sensory word   *Grades:* 3 and up
Play Method: Individual or team, written or oral

As a written or oral individual game: As an oral game, ask players at random to give a sentence that complies with the rules of the game. As a written game, have each player write the required sentence. Then call on each player in turn to read his sentence.

As a written team game: Divide the group into teams. Let each group choose a captain. At the signal to begin, the captain assigns a sense—touch, sight, hearing, taste, or smell—to each player, repeating the sequence if necessary. He assigns one to himself, as well. At the signal, each player writes his required sentence and hands it to the captain. If a player is bogged down, a teammate may help him. Allow five minutes or less. When time is up have each team read its list and permit time for comment.

Reading Directions

We learn through our five senses, touch, sight, hearing, taste, and smell. If we want to tell others what we have learned, we cannot just say, "I ate an apple," and expect them to know much about what it was like to eat that apple. Now, if we say, "My apple was sour," the listener can understand better what we had experienced. Our game is a sentence-making game. The sentence must contain a word describing a particular sense experience we have had. I will give you an example for each of the five senses to show you how this game works.

> *Touch:* My bed was soft and warm.
> *Hearing:* The police siren screamed and wailed.
> *Sight:* The sky was blue with puffy white clouds.
> *Taste:* My chocolate milk was sweet and cold.
> *Smell:* I smelled bacon frying when I woke up.

If you can't think of something to write about, just look around the room and you will see, hear, smell, and be able to touch something you can write a sentence about. The taste sentence should not be hard. Think of your favorite foods and the rest should be easy.

Reading Directions

Variation: What we see or smell, touch, hear, or see makes us feel some way inside. We may feel good, unhappy, sick, sorry, or wonderful. If you want to add how you felt inside when you make up your sentences, try to think how you might have felt if you had really seen or heard, felt, smelled, or tasted a particular thing. Add a word that tells us something about your feelings. Then we can understand what you are saying better.

I will read the same examples I gave you before, but I will have added some other words. See how that word helps us to feel the same feelings the sentence writer had.

Touch: My bed was soft and warm and I felt snug and safe.

Hearing: The police siren screamed and wailed and made me feel afraid.

Sight: The sky was blue with puffy white clouds. It was beautiful.

Taste: My chocolate milk was sweet and cold and tasted just wonderful.

Smell: I smelled bacon frying when I woke up. It made my mouth water.

SENSITIVE DESCRIPTIONS

Type of Game: Sensory word   *Grades:* 3 and up
Play Method: Oral or written individual

As an oral game: With younger children, have the players volunteer answers, which should then be written on the board.

As a written game: Give the class words and have each player make in a limited time, a written list describing the words. At the end of the time limit, call on each player for a description.

Reading Directions

There are words that accurately describe things we see, things we hear, things we touch, taste, and smell. Through our senses we learn about some things as we could learn about them in no other way. No one can really tell us how vanilla tastes. No one can accurately describe the color red to a blind person.

When you really think about it, we seldom have an experience that involves only one sense. For example, let's take peanut butter. We see it. It has a certain beige or light brown color. We spread it, so we experience its texture. It may be sticky, chunky, oily, or thick. So our sense of touch is involved. We smell its nutty, peanut flavor, and we taste it. We have another sensation, our reaction to it. We either like it or we find it sickening because we don't like it. So with peanut butter, four senses are involved—and so is an emotion.

Take another word—dog. For each sense involved we can find picture words that describe a particular dog. He might be black and white (sight), silky-haired (touch), have a high shrill bark (sound), and smell strongly of fertilizer he has been rolling in (smell). Described in that manner, we can give a clear picture of this dog to others. Add to this your personal reaction, and the listeners would know your personal reaction to him. You may have been disgusted because you know you will have to bathe him. Or you may have been overjoyed to see him because he had been gone for some time and you thought he was lost.

In this game I will give you a word, such as *house*, or a phrase. How many different senses can you involve in describing it? Then, for each sense, find the best picture or descriptive word you can so that we can "see" this house with you. All of us will not see the same house, so before we are finished, we should have many different pictures. After some descriptions you may want to add your personal reaction word—how it makes you feel.

Teacher Reference List

apple	money	schoolroom
cat	garbage can	Chanukah
house	newspaper	mountains
dog	Christmas	bowl of chili

parakeet	party	hamburger sandwich
home	seashore	potato chip
popcorn	church	motion picture theater
new baseball mitt	a sleep-out	typewriter
new shoes	guitar	tennis shoe
hospital	gymnasium	low-flying jet
soap	hot summer day	new automobile
milk	television	bag of books
campfire	fire	rainstorm
chocolate cake	bread	school bus
sub-zero day	rose	Halloween
zoo	watermelon	walk in the woods
thunderstorm		

Note: Encourage players to think up other words to suggest for future games.

SIGHT WORD GAME

Type of Game: Sensory word   *Grades:* 3 and up
Method of Play: Individual or team, oral or written

As a written or oral individual game: As an oral game, call on the players either at random as they volunteer or in rotation.

As an individual written game: Present the problem and give the players time to write a list. At the end of the time period, call on players in rotation to give examples.

As a written team game: Organize the players into teams, each with a captain-secretary who records the suggestions of his teammates and adds his own contributions as well. At the end of the time period, call on each captain in turn to give five words. Write on the board, under the classifications suggested in the reading directions.

Reading Directions

In this game we are playing with words that describe things we have seen. *Sight* words are what we will call them. Just to say that something is "pretty" or "horrible" is not accurate enough to convey what we saw to another person. What we want to do is let that person see what we saw so clearly that he almost sees it with us. An accurate description may help you learn the identity of something. For example, to say, "I saw a beautiful bird today," tells the listener nothing except that you saw a bird and thought it beautiful. But suppose you were to say, "I saw a red bird with a topknot. He had a yellow beak and a black spot just behind it. He was about eight or nine inches long. Not as big as a robin." This gives a very clear picture. Anyone who knows birds could identify it for you as a cardinal.

The sight words we are playing with today describe the things we see. They describe color, shape, size, appearance, rate of speed, kind of movement, and a state of being such as new, broken, or dirty. And, in addition, to many sight experiences we have, we have some kind of reaction. We may find such an experience sad, beautiful, sickening, or inspiring.

If the captain writes these classifications across the top of a page, he can then write words as they are given to him under their proper classifications. Players giving the words should tell the captain where they belong. To repeat, these are the classifications: color (red, yellow); shape (round, stringy); size (enormous, tiny); appearance (wet, smooth); rate of speed (racing, motionless); kind of movement (dancing, racing); state of being (new, dirty). Don't forget the reaction words, which tell how what you saw made you feel. These would be words like *exciting, beautiful, ugly*.

To get started, think about a favorite possession or something you saw on the way to school today that interested you. Find as many words to describe this sight as you can. Ready?

Teacher Reference List

Color	Size	Shape	Appearance
red	tiny	round	rough
green	bulky	spindly	sandy
blue	tall	oval	smooth
pink	jumbo	roly-poly	spiked
lavender	gigantic	cubiform	velvety
purple	enormous	rectangular	watery
black	stunted	twisted	satiny
white	minute	curved	slippery
orange	imposing	triangular	woven
turquoise	teeny	pentagonal	braided
mixed	unlimited	pyramidal	prickly
calico	half-sized	octagonal	rocky
brindled	full-sized	cylindrical	concrete
gray	pint-sized	irregular	stony
brown	magnified	snakelike	gritty
yellow	limitless	hook-shaped	dusty
pale	graduated	arched	slushy
tinted	immense	egg-shaped	feathery
pastel	colossal	granular	wet
multi-colored	king-sized		sharp

Rate of Speed	Kind of Movement	State of Being	Reaction
quick	graceful	unfinished	horrible
slow	awkward	crowded	welcome
halting	violent	broken	funny
limping	on all fours	empty	sad
dragging	limping	new	shocking

Rate of Speed	Kind of Movement	State of Being	Reaction
crawling	weakly	half-full	beautiful
hurrying	jerkily	decayed	inspiring
fleet	step by step	rotten	hilarious
lively	painfully	braced	breathtaking
hurried	in circles	leaning	satisfying
running	clumsily	whole	amazing
rushed	dancing	collapsed	astonishing
spilling over	sidewise	deteriorated	unbelievable
bounding	trippingly	burned	depressing
speedy	trotting	scorched	uplifting
racing	loping	ripped	forbidding
rapid	sprinting	melted	incredible
brisk	whirling	torn	sickening
dashing	on tiptoe	frozen	amusing
hastily	scampering	shredded	heart-warming
like wildfire	galloping	melting	
pell-mell	soaring	dirty	
presto	winging	dripping	
spurt	hovering	sparkling clean	
accelerated	gliding	sunburned	
like a shot	slipping	foggy	

Variation: Give the players something to describe. After a limited time call on volunteers to read their descriptions. It will be interesting to the players to see how many different kinds of sight descriptions are possible. Examples of possible sight experiences to describe are given below. Emphasize that the sight words are the ones that are to be used, even though everyone understands that most experiences involve more than one sense.

Teacher Reference List

a thunderstorm	the school building
an elephant	a school bus
a heavy snowstorm	a new dress or new suit
a beautiful day	a favorite toy or possession
litter	a campfire
a birthday cake	something in the classroom

SOUND WORDS

Type of Game: Sensory word   *Grades:* 3 and up
Play Method: Oral individual or written team

As an oral individual game: Ask for words volunteered by players in the group and write them on the board, the player suggesting the word spelling it out.

As a written team game: Divide the group into teams, with a secretary-captain for each. The captain writes down the words suggested by his teammates and adds his own contributions as well. Allow about five minutes for writing time. Each team then reads its list. Score a point for a correct word and an extra point if correctly spelled. The team with the most points wins.

Reading Directions

We learn through our five senses, hearing, smell, taste, touch, and sight. There are words that describe the sounds we hear, some more accurately than others. If we are describing something we heard to others and want them to "hear" these sounds as we heard them, then we must be careful in our selection of words. For example, to say, "I heard a funny sound today that frightened me," only tells people how the sound affected you or what your reaction to it was, but it tells nothing about the kind of sound it was. Now if you were to say, "Suddenly there was a loud explosion that shook the whole building and I was scared stiff," we would know exactly what kind of sound frightened you, as well as your reaction to it.

Sound words can be divided into bird sounds (twittering, cheeping); animal sounds (mooing, barking); people sounds (yelling, talking); thing sounds (sonic boom, police siren, drumming); quality of sound (harsh, monotonous, stealthy); personal reactions (frightening, soothing, restful).

The captain will write these classifications across the top of a page. When a teammate gives a word, he can write it under a particular classification. If you think of a particular sound and the way it makes you feel, you will be able to give your captain two words, the sound word itself and your reaction to it. For example, think of the school bell. What kind of sound does it make and how do you feel when you hear it? As another example, consider the fire-drill bell. You will find it easier if you think of a particular thing and the sound it makes. It will be easy then to find the word that describes it and maybe even your usual reaction to that sound.

Teacher Reference List

Birds	Animals	People
cooing	mooing	boohooing
cawing	lowing	sneezing
twittering	baying	coughing
cuckooing	bleating	gargling
screeching	grunting	talking
honking	purring	moaning
quacking	snoring	grunting
crowing	whinnying	groaning
calling	growling	shuffling
peeping	rattling	slapping

Birds	*Animals*	*People*
squawking	howling	murmuring
chattering	scratching	kissing
fluttering	coughing	puffing
chirping	roaring	cooing
cheeping	squealing	yelling
cackling	licking	screaming
gobbling	buzzing	clapping
pecking	thumping	whooping
scolding	trumpeting	singing
trilling	panting	slurping
warbling	yawning	raving
scratching	bellowing	sipping
whistling	caterwauling	smacking
	squeaking	chewing
		wailing
		giggling
		laughing

Things	*Quality*	*Personal Reaction*
whistling	liquid	beautiful
crashing	soft	breathtaking
rattling	characteristic	unbelievable
hammering	loud	painful
roaring (motor)	resonant	harmonious
ticking	vibrating	ear-splitting
bonging	monotonous	obnoxious
ringing	throaty	lovely
exploding	sonorous	magnificent
blowing	rhythmic	exasperating
howling (winds)	stealthy	joyful
screaming (sirens)	frightened	glorious
clanking	stereophonic	shocking

Things	Quality	Personal Reaction
tooting	melodic	superb
burning	anxious	appalling
crackling	shrill	jarring
blasting	raspy	agreeable
humming	flowing	maddening
dripping	recurrent	horrid
chugging	discordant	hideous
thundering	clear	meaningless
muffled	mournful	soothing
musical	quavering	sweet
drumming	weird	blissful
twanging	flat	pleasing
	faint	pleasant
	plaintive	

TASTY WORDS

Type of Game: Sensory word   Grades: 3 and up
Play Method: Oral individual game or written team game

As an oral individual game: Ask for volunteer answers and write them on the blackboard.

As a written team game: Organize the group into teams, each with a captain-secretary who records his teammates' answers and contributes his own as well. Allow three to five minutes for teams to compile lists, then call on the captains, in turn, to read their lists. Write the words on the blackboard to avoid duplications, as well as to show the variety possible.

Reading Directions

We learn through our five senses, smell, taste, hearing, touch, and sight. The feelings we have are called sensations. There are words to describe our many feelings. The more words we know and use, the better we are able to communicate with others so that they know exactly what experiences we are talking about. For example, it is not enough to say, "The food tastes bad," and expect a person to know what you mean. He needs to know what you mean by "bad." You may think the food is not good because it is too peppery. But your friends may like peppery food, so they would not think it bad-tasting at all. So, to give your impression exactly, you must use words that really let others know what sensation you are experiencing.

In this game we are playing with taste words. Let's see how many we can list in five minutes. To get started, think of some food you like very much or dislike. Try to find words that tell why you like or dislike that particular food.

Teacher Reference List

sweet	nutty	aromatic	chocolate,
oversweet	greasy	flavorful	strawberry, etc.)
bitter	lukewarm	racy	smoky
refreshing	rotten	rancid	moist
cool	tasty	tasteless	tangy
fizzy	minty	juicy	cheesy
tart	yummy	sugared	garlicky
spicy	tart	syrupy	sharp
cold	tinny	vinegary	raw
hot (peppery)	poisonous	winey	tasteless
salty	nauseous	rank	savory
gritty	burnt	fresh	gingery
sandy	insipid	stale	doughy
fermented	oniony	mushy	overripe
spoiled	sugary	dry	overcooked
green or unripe	saccharine	undercooked	bloody
mouth-watering	candied	flavored	
sickening	pungent	(vanilla,	

Variation #1: One player with a particular adjective in mind gives an incomplete sentence such as: "I don't like this meat because it is (tough)." The other players volunteer answers until the correct word is named. The player guessing the correct word gives the next sentence. The sentences should be limited to foods to limit the field of words.

Variation #2: Play as a spell-down game. Divide the group into two teams, alternating from team to team in rotation. Each player must name a taste word. A player who cannot name one (keep a list to avoid duplications) sits down. Play until all the members of one team are eliminated.

TOUCH WORDS

Type of Game: Word   *Grades:* 3 and up
Play Method: Oral or written, team or individual

As an oral game: Challenge the group with the game problem. Select a volunteer from the group at random or take a volunteer from each team alternately, scoring correct answers on a team basis.

As a written game: Divide the group into teams with a secretary-captain. The captain records the words volunteered by his teammates and makes his own contributions as well. At the end of five minutes have each team read its list. Score a point for each correct word and an extra point if it is correctly spelled.

Reading Directions

We learn through our five senses, smell, taste, hearing, sight, and touch. The words we are going to play with in this game are those dealing with the sense of touch. Just to say something felt "awful" does not tell a listener anything about the object touched except that the sensation experienced by the person touching the object was not a happy one and may even have been frightening. Now if someone were to say, "It felt cold and clammy to my touch, causing shivers to run up my back," the listeners would have a fair idea of why the toucher was repelled by the object.

Words dealing with the sense of touch have to do with texture (rough, smooth); movement (motionless, wiggly); shape (round, egg-shaped); temperature (scorching, icy); degree of dryness or moistness (arid, dripping).

We must remember, too, that for every sensory experience—an experience we have with one sense or another—we have a particular feeling or reaction. We react to it, in other words. We feel happy, sad, angry, frightened, or uncomfortable. We call these feelings *emotional reactions*, and in this game we will call them *reaction words*.

Before we begin, each captain will write the classifications across the top of his page in this manner: *shape, texture, movement, temperature, degree of dryness or moistness,* and *reaction words.* These classifications will help you find the words more easily. Anyone on the team may suggest a word to the captain and tell him under which classification it comes. For example, you may be thinking of a wiggly worm. If you have ever touched or held a worm, you know it felt cool, wet, and wiggly. So you could be giving your captain three words if you described a worm that way. If it made you feel squeamish, then you are giving a reaction word at the same time.

The easiest way to think of touch words is to imagine something or really touch something in your pocket or close to you and then think of words to describe how it feels to you.

We have five minutes to make lists. Each team will get a point for a correct touch word and another point if it is spelled correctly. The team with the most points wins. Ready? Go!

Teacher Reference List

Texture

scratchy
furry
scaly
sharp
rough
dull
silky
bony
satiny
paper-smooth
velvety
knotty
spongy
grainy
mossy
springy
crumbly
porous
granular
holey
sandy
slippery
muddy
crinkled
sticky
hard
fragile
soft
peachlike
powdery

dusty
netlike
cobweb-like
papery
doughy
mucky
sawtoothed
shocking
  (electrical)

Shape

round
square
cube
egglike
stringy
cylindrical
ropelike
flat
wavy
beadlike

Movement

convulsive
flowing
rushing
wiggly
slithering
slow
frantic
steady
intermittent
sudden
in circles
spinning
stirring
creeping
rolling
rhythmic
hopping
jiggling
twitching
fidgety
restless
flopping
shaky

Temperature

scorching hot
chilly
freezing cold
shocking cold
lukewarm
burning hot
frigid
toasty hot
warm
cool
boiling hot
biting cold
blistering cold
searing hot
fiery
steamy hot
wintry
balmy
benumbing
congealing

Degree of Dryness or Moistness	Reaction
dewy	snug
slimy	cozy
moist	painful
soggy	feverish
bone dry	satisfying
wringing wet	frightening
dry as dust	exciting
thick and sticky	desperate
half melted	refreshing
steamy	sensuous
foamy	strange
bubbly	distressing
soapy	uncomfortable
sudsy	unpleasant
misty	curious
frothy	thrilling
drizzling	startling
pouring	bizarre
driving rain	agreeable
pelting hail	indescribable
driven snow	

WORDS OF SMELL

Type of Game: Sensory word   Grades: 3 and up
Play Method: Oral individual or written team

As an oral individual game: Challenge the players to volunteer and spell words, which are then written on the blackboard.

As a written team game: Divide the group into teams, each with a captain-secretary who writes the words suggested by his teammates and adds his own as well. After the game is explained, allow five minutes for teams to compile lists, then allow time for teams to read their lists. Score a point for an acceptable word and an extra point if it is correctly spelled. If you call for one word from each team in turn, interest will be kept high.

Reading Directions

We learn through our five senses of sight, smell, taste, hearing, and touch. There are words to describe the sensations we experience through each of these senses. The more carefully we select the words we use in describing something we have learned through the sense of smell the more we can communicate to another person what we have experienced. Just to say that something smells "terrible" does not really convey what the smell was like except that we found it disagreeable. Now if I were to say, "The earth smelled fresh and clean after a night-long rain," you would know exactly what I had experienced, particularly if you had had a similar experience.

I will give you hints of the kinds of words we are looking for. There are smells we associate with animals (skunks); people (sweat); things (singed, fragrant); places (fried onions, hamburgers); nature (pines, cabbage fields). We should remember that people often take on the smells of things they work with. Thus a painter might smell of paint or a fry-cook of onions and hot grease.

One more thing to remember is that the experiences we have through the sense of smell affect us in one way or another. If we smell something we like, we find it pleasing or mouth-watering. Such words are often used alone with descriptive smell words. So we will include this type of words in with the other types.

If you think this is difficult, just think of a pet, your favorite food, or your favorite flower. This will help you to find words associated with smell.

The captains will write the words players on their teams suggest. Let's see how many different words we can find in five minutes.

Teacher Reference List

acrid	fragrant	musky	rotten
antiseptic	freshly laundered	musty	sawdust,
beery	fruity	nauseous	new lumber
bitter	funereal	nose-stinging	savory
burnt	garlicky	nose-tickling	sharp
cheesy	gaseous	offensive	sickening
chlorinated	gingery	oily	singed
dank	fresh green	onion	skunk-like
disgusting	herby	fresh paint	slight
dusty	hircine	perfumed	smokey
enticing	(like a goat)	piney	sour
evil-smelling	incense	poisonous	spicy
fermented	lavender	pungent	tangy
fetid	medicinal	putrid	vinegary
fishy	minty	rancid	yeasty
flowery	moldy	rank	zoo-like
foul	mouth-watering	repulsive	

Variation: Give key words such as hamburger stand or locker room and give the teams one minute to list smells they associate with such places.

Teacher Reference List

bus on a rainy day	hospital
campfire	movie house
carnival	pizza parlor
circus	woods in spring or fall
classroom	zoo
favorite smells	

Antonyms and Synonyms

ANTONYM NAME-DOWN

Type of Game: Word   Grades: 4 and up
Play Method: Oral team game
  Organize into two teams, as for a spell-down.

Reading Directions

  This is a game in which we will play with antonyms—words
that mean the opposite of another word. For example, take the
word firm. Antonyms or opposites of that word are *unstable,
shaky, unsteady*. Take another example, the word *strong*. Antonyms are *weak, feeble, infirm*, and *frail*.

  We will play this game in spell-down style except that a
player who misses a word is not eliminated but will cause an
error point to be scored against his team. We will begin with
the first player of team 1. I will give a word and that player will
try to name an antonym. If he cannot do so or names an incorrect word, his team scores an error point and the first player
of team 2 will try to give an antonym for that word. After
two correct antonyms have been named, I will ask players of
both teams to volunteer another antonym for the same word.
A correct word named erases an error, but mistakes in these
volunteered words will be counted as errors. If a team has no
errors to erase when a correct extra word is given, a credit point
will be given to be used later to erase an error.

  After all extra words have been volunteered, I will give a new
word and the next player whose regular turn was coming up will
begin. The team with the lowest number of errors wins the
game. Ready?

Note: With older children play for three or four antonyms
before changing words. In the event of a challenge, have all

players consult their dictionaries, or the teacher can consult hers
and be the final authority.

Teacher Reference List

Word	Antonyms
vain	modest, humble, shy, unassuming
modern	antique, obsolete, out-of-date, old-fashioned
large	small, little, tiny, petty, insignificant
afraid	brave, bold, self-controlled, fearless, cool, valiant, composed
brave	craven, cowardly, afraid, timid, shy
evil	good, goodness, holy, righteous, virtue, esteem
bright	dark, gloomy, cloudy, shady, dull, murky, dreary
busy	idle, indolent, lazy, motionless, inactive
careful	careless, negligent, heedless, imprudent, thoughtless
ease	worry, sorrow, trouble, discomfort, unrest, turmoil
firm	weak, unstable, unsettled, untied, wobbling
quiet	noisy, loud, deafening, ear-splitting
difficult	easy, facile, simple, free, unconstrained, tranquil
attack	defend, resist, guard, protect, shelter, shield
have	lack, want, need, be short of
haste	slowness, tardiness, delay, tarrying, ease, lateness
succeed	fail, lose, forfeit, miss, blunder, trip
mirth	sadness, melancholy, grief, unhappiness, sorrow
pretty	ugly, homely, common, ordinary, repulsive, dowdy
strong	weak, frail, feeble, infirm
separate	adhere, cohere, cling, cleave
stiff	pliant, flexible, limp, limber
strange	common, commonplace, ordinary, expected, trite, usual
stupid	quick, sharp, keen, alert, comprehending, wide-awake, brainy
yield	conquer, vanquish
prejudice	appreciation, admiration, esteem, respect, consideration

precise	inexact, faulty, slipshod, erring, misleading
true	false, fickle, lying, imaginary, disloyal, fictional
trust	mistrust, doubt, discredit, disbelief, misgiving
unequal	equal, balanced, even, same, matched, regular, constant
uneasy	steady, firm, sober, constant, quiet, content
want	plenty, riches, wealth, abundance, affluence, luxury
wait	anticipate, forestall, hurry, quicken, accelerate
violent	gentle, mild, tender, soft, kind, kindly, restful
wisdom	folly, foolishness, silliness, senselessness, error
work	idleness, ease, leisure, relaxation, recreation
racket	peace, quietude, truce, concord, harmony
quit	remain, retain, hold, keep, occupy, guard, watch
quick	slow, creeping, tardy, languid, snail-like, weary, indolent
motionless	moving, shifting, changing, restless, traveling
learn	teach, guide, inform, instruct, coach, direct, enlighten
monotonous	varied, versatile, interesting, lively, refreshing
ingenious	unskilled, unskillful, bungling, blundering, incompetent
influence	unimportance, uselessness, powerlessness, inferiority
incite	deter, hold back, dissuade, check, dampen, discourage
humane	barbarous, atrocious, savage, pitiless, inhuman, cruel
hope	hopelessness, despair, dejection, pessimism, discouragement
grudge	goodwill, friendliness, brotherliness, kindness
wrong	right, goodness, justice, honesty, integrity
tough	mild, gentle, yielding, composed, modest
thick	thin, foamy, frothy, scarce, sparse
stern	gentle, kind, considerate, lenient, indulgent, easy
popular	hateful, odious, detestable, repulsive, shunned, repellent
object	like, desire, want, wish, implore, entreat
liberty	slavery, oppression, compulsion, confinement

Variation #1: Play as a read-and-write game. Write a numbered list of words on the blackboard and have the players write antonyms, numbering them as on the board. At the end of the time limit, call on players in rotation.

Variation #2: Play as a team read-and-write game, in which players on each team pool their ideas. At the end of the time limit, call on teams in turn. For every correct word, score a point. The team with the highest number of points wins.

SYNONYM NAME-DOWN

Type of Game: Word   *Grades:*   4 and up
Play Method: Oral team spell-down

Organize the group into two teams, as for a spell-down.

Reading Directions

This is a game in which we will play with synonyms—words that mean the same as another or can be used in place of another. As a joke, someone once said that a synonym is a word we use when we can't spell or pronounce the word we intended to use. In this game we will try to find several ways of saying the same thing. For example, take the word *weak.* Synonyms for it are *infirm, feeble, frail, decrepit.* Consider the word *rich* and some of its synonyms—*wealthy, affluent, opulent, well-to-do.*

We will play this game in spell-down style. I will name a word and the first player of the first team will try to name a synonym. If he can, I will call on the first player of the second team to give another. If a player cannot give a correct word, he scores an error for his team and the player on the next team gets a chance. After two synonyms have been correctly named for a word, I will call for volunteers out of turn to name another.

If a player gives a correct word, he can erase an error from his team score. But if he volunteers an incorrect word, he scores an error. This extra part of the play helps a team to erase its errors, but it can score against your team, too, so be sure before you volunteer. If a team has no errors when an extra word is given, a credit point is scored to be used later against an error. If there are no volunteers for extra words, I will name a new word and play will begin with the player whose turn was coming up. The team with the lowest score at the end wins. Ready?

Note: Consult a dictionary in the event of a questionable word.

Teacher Reference List

Word	Synonyms
young	youthful, juvenile, adolescent, vigorous, early
large	big, great, vast, immense, huge
afraid	frightened, timid, timorous, fearful, terrified
aggressive	militant, pushing, assertive
distress	suffering, agony, anguish, misery, pain
distribute	allot, dole, dispense, divide, share
boil	seethe, simmer, stew
border	margin, edge, rim, brim, brink
branch	bough, twig, offshoot, limb
brave	unafraid, courageous, bold, audacious, plucky
break	smash, crash, shatter, crack, fracture, splinter, split
bright	radiant, shining, brilliant, luminous, lustrous
bundle	package, parcel, pack, bale
burn	scorch, singe, sear, char
busy	industrious, diligent, involved, active
call	summon, invite, convene, convoke
careful	meticulous, scrupulous, prudent, wary, cautious, accurate
carry	bear, convey, transmit, transport

Word	Synonyms
catch	capture, nab, trap, snare
cause	reason, motive, effect, induce
change	alter, transform, modify, vary, convert
choice	alternative, option, preference, selection, superior
ease	quiet, rest, repose, comfort
firm	solid, hard, stiff, fixed, stable
difficult	arduous, baffling, hard, complex, tough
attack	beset, assault, storm, bombard, assail
have	hold, own, possess, control
mirth	glee, merriment, hilarity, laughter
sport	pastime, diversion, play
strong	tough, powerful, sturdy, robust, hale, muscular
stick	adhere, cohere, cling, cleave
stiff	rigid, inflexible, firm, tense
succeed	flourish, prosper, thrive, follow
pretty	attractive, beautiful, comely, sightly, beauteous
still	noiseless, hushed, silent, motionless
prejudice	bigotry, discrimination, bias, slant, unfairness
evil	bad, wicked, corrupt, foul, unholy, vile, unrighteous
love	devotion, affection, fondness, reverence, adoration
take	capture, accept, appropriate, seize
trap	snare, catch, pitfall, ambush
new	fresh, novel, modern, original, recent
build	erect, construct, put up, raise, make, establish
bravery	courage, valor, daring, spunk, boldness, spirit, fortitude
narrow	restricted, cramped, close, contracted, limited, scanty
rational	wise, sensible, sane, reasonable, sound, logical
support	maintain, uphold, sustain, keep, carry, cherish
want	lack, need, privation, hunger, penniless
thankless	ungrateful, insensible, grumbling, discontented, dissatisfied
give	donate, grant, compensate, contribute
learn	acquire, gain, receive, study, read, follow

short	incomplete, brief, concise, abridged, abbreviated, stunted, dwarfed, stocky, compact
punish	chastise, whip, correct, spank, strike
provoke	rouse, excite, stir, move, incite, enrage, taunt, anger
miserable	unhappy, pained, distressed, sick, ailing, friendless
method	order, system, arrangement, style, manner, vogue, routine
important	significant, relevant, essential, serious, determining
imperative	urgent, authoritative, irresistible, obligatory, essential
impartial	fair, just, unbiased, right, good, equal, reasonable
imitate	copy, mimic, ape, mock, counterfeit, duplicate, simulate
exempt	free, clear, liberated, excused, excluded, privileged
expense	cost, price, outlay, charge, payment, outgo, disbursement
excite	rouse, stir up, provoke, awaken, incite, arouse

Note: With younger players, ask for fewer synonyms and use the simpler words.

Variation: Play as a read-and-write game. Write a numbered list of words on the blackboard and have the players write the synonyms, numbering them in the same order. Call on players at random and ask for selections. Allow time for discussion and correction.

Index

177